NEW DIRECTIONS FOR COMMUNITY COLLEGES

Arthur M. Cohen
EDITOR-IN-CHIEF

Florence B. Brawer
ASSOCIATE EDITOR

Organizational Change in the Community College: A Ripple or a Sea Change?

John Stewart Levin
University of Arizona

EDITOR

Number 102, Summer 1998

JOSSEY-BASS PUBLISHERS
San Francisco

ιity Colleges

ORGANIZATIONAL CHANGE IN THE COMMUNITY COLLEGE:
A RIPPLE OR A SEA CHANGE?
John S. Levin (ed.)
New Directions for Community Colleges, no. 102
Volume XXVI, number 2
Arthur M. Cohen, Editor-in-Chief
Florence B. Brawer, Associate Editor

New Directions for Community Colleges is indexed in Current Index to Journals in Education (ERIC).

Microfilm copies of issues and articles are available in 16mm and 35mm, as well as microfiche in 105mm, through University Microfilms Inc., 300 North Zeeb Road, Ann Arbor, Michigan 48106-1346.

ISSN 0194-3081   ISBN 0-7879-4235-9

NEW DIRECTIONS FOR COMMUNITY COLLEGES is part of the Jossey-Bass Higher and Adult Education Series and is published quarterly by Jossey-Bass Inc., Publishers, 350 Sansome Street, San Francisco, California 94104-1342, in association with the ERIC Clearinghouse for Community Colleges. ERIC is sponsored by the U.S. Department of Education, Office of Educational Research and Improvement, and is administered by the National Library of Education. Periodicals postage paid at San Francisco, California, and at additional mailing offices. POSTMASTER: Send address changes to New Directions for Community Colleges, Jossey-Bass Inc., Publishers, 350 Sansome Street, San Francisco, California 94104-1342.

SUBSCRIPTIONS cost $57.00 for individuals and $107.00 for institutions, agencies, and libraries. Prices subject to change.

THE MATERIAL in this publication is based on work sponsored wholly or in part by the Office of Educational Research and Improvement, U.S. Department of Education, under contract number RI-93-00-2003. Its contents do not necessarily reflect the views of the Department or any other agency of the U.S. Government.

EDITORIAL CORRESPONDENCE should be sent to the Editor-in-Chief, Arthur M. Cohen, at the ERIC Clearinghouse for Community Colleges, University of California, 3051 Moore Hall, 405 Hilgard Avenue, Los Angeles, California 90024–1521.

Cover photograph © Rene Sheret, After Image, Los Angeles, California, 1990.

www.josseybass.com

CONTENTS

Organizational change is a complex concept, suggesting various perspectives of organization. For the community college, organizational change can be viewed as a process that defines the identity of the institution.

Organizational Change and the Community College

John Stewart Levin

Organizational change is both multifaceted and complex. Levy and Merry (1986) suggest that organizational change has several discrete characteristics, such as alteration to organizational purpose and alteration to organizational processes. These characteristics identify or classify the nature or type of change in an organization. Others look to the forces or sources of change that affect organizations (for example, Pfeffer, 1982), treating the organization as an object on which action is taken. And those attempting to influence practitioners by guiding them through change processes view organizational change as a strategy to help the organization adapt to its environment—for example, justifying managerial behaviors in leading organizational action.

Too often, higher education literature, especially community college literature, focuses on change as a panacea for problems or as a synonym for innovation, suggesting that change has positive qualities and few negative ones. Although this perspective can be supported by empirical evidence, there is also a need for perspectives of change that suggest greater complexity and conflict than cases of exemplary practice. In this volume, several sides of organizational change in the community college are depicted so that practitioners and scholars can gain a more comprehensive view of organizational behaviors.

What ties these various perspectives together? I suggest that these perspectives depend on viewers' understandings of the community college and their definition of its identity as an institution. The purposes of the institution, the meaning of its behaviors and actions, and its public social and educational roles constitute its identity. That identity is the basis on which we—practitioners and observers—understand and explain organizational change. Those who accept the identity of the community college as a socially transforming institution will in turn see and articulate change in the organization in the social transformation context, observing, for example, that the principle of access to education is practiced by community colleges and results in the provision of opportunities to millions of people. Thus, altering organizational structures to serve the ends of access is not only to be expected but also to be praised by those who connect the identity of the community college to access.

In this volume, there are numerous understandings of the community college. There are both bleak views of governance and management and optimistic views about college responsiveness to community needs. Through descriptions of organizational actions in the form of organizational change, we are able to see the multiple identities of the community college.

I make the assumption that the essential nature of the community college, its identity, is embedded in what it does: in its actions and change processes. Thus, the organization's responses to external stimuli, its adaptation to its environment, the behaviors of its members, and the social and political dynamics in and surrounding the institution are expressions of organization and efforts to not only maintain but also reproduce its identity. In short, the actions of the community college arise from its identity and express its identity.

If we assume that organizations are living entities, or at least composed of living beings, then as living systems change, movement, even a state of flux, is a given: organizational behaviors are not static, behaviors beget actions, and actions translate into change. Change may be the product of tensions between oppositions, as in Marxist or neo-Marxist theory, or it may be the product of organizational maintenance or self-reproduction (Morgan, 1986). Organizations are not static: they change, metaphorically growing, expanding, contracting, and eventually dying. And what they do in all of these processes is define and express themselves: by their actions they are known.

What, then, are community colleges? Unlike four-year colleges and universities, community colleges are nontraditional or untraditional: they do not even adhere to their own traditions (Cohen and Brawer, 1989). They make and remake themselves.

The efforts of community colleges to don the garb of traditional organizations, especially those entrenched in the historical and the symbolic, are destined to alter the dress code. Take, for example, shared governance in California community colleges (see Chapter Three). Reflective of a collegial and historical environment, shared governance stands on the assumption of a community of scholars (Goodman, 1962), an idealized image of the academy. Such an image is unspoiled by adversarial relations of collective bargaining or by political conflicts in a pluralistic environment. But the idealized image does not last long in the community college. Not only is the institution affected by shared governance, but also the concept of shared governance itself is transformed: shared governance in California community colleges looks nothing like a community of scholars; instead, conflict and adversarial relations have seized the day (see Chapter Three).

The community college, both institution and movement, not only alters itself to adapt and survive but also adopts what is not itself to incorporate the new, integrating other with self. Shared governance is acquired from four-year colleges and universities, Total Quality Management and corporate mergers are borrowed from business, and multiculturalism is adopted from national and international social movements (see Chapters Four and Six). Because of its very nature, including responsiveness, open access for students, unicameral governance (one domain of authority), and untraditionality, the community college is an institution of choice not only for a large sector of the college population but also as a target for social and economic policy, such as the Clinton administration's welfare-to-work and workforce policies. The multiple functions and broad mission of the community college have no doubt made the institution susceptible to change as well as a receptacle of educational trends, from learning paradigms to assessment movements. This predisposition to change also shows us that broad social movements and national and regional cultures are part of the community college's environment. The several striking features of the community college, including its characteristic of internalizing its environment, may indeed be part of the borderless world of postmodern organizations (see Chapter Nine). This does not mean, however, that the community college is susceptible to identity loss, but rather that its responsive and adaptive qualities, its malleability and its proclivity to embrace practice not theory, action not reflection, are defining features of its identity.

What, then, is not acceptable to the community college? At what point will it refuse to bend, and maintain if not its traditions then its habits and values? First, the community college cannot be ahead of the pack. Although it can incorporate trends, it does not set them. Perhaps the institution as described by Pepicello and Hopkins (Chapter Seven) is more a mirror of society than a lamp that illuminates the way. Although the institution possesses democratic and socialist features—for example, its emphasis on equality of opportunity— it does not adopt a radical or anticapitalistic position, such as an approach taken by socialist feminists to eliminate gender oppression (see Chapter Eight). This suggests that although change is a defining characteristic of the community college, the change is neither revolutionary nor deep enough to challenge the values of the organization's members or constituents. In this sense, the community college acts and changes in accord with its identity, and organizational changes are elaborations of that identity. This may explain why the Minnesota higher education merger is viewed as a catastrophe by Wallace (Chapter Two), because such a change is not consistent with either Wallace's or his Minnesota colleagues' understandings of the community college. The same could be said for White (Chapter Three) and his denunciation of shared governance in California.

We are not necessarily experiencing a sea change, a radical transformation of the institution. But perhaps we are observing a clear picture of the community college: the kind of institution it is, both untraditional and social as well as educational, and its foremost characteristics of adaptability and dynamism.

As a living system, the community college acts and changes in order to express its nature and to survive.

The following chapters express this identity through exploration of organizational change. They look at change through a variety of lenses: through managerial actions, through state system policy and actions, through institutional effects on minority students, through the understandings of a large cross section of institutional members, and through feminist and postmodern frameworks. We can certainly learn from these explorations that the community college is a complicated institution, with its behaviors subject to a variety of interpretations, and its actions tied to its multiple purposes, roles, and constituents.

References

Cohen, A. M., and Brawer, F. B. *The American Community College.* (2nd ed.) San Francisco: Jossey-Bass, 1989.

Goodman, P. *The Community of Scholars.* New York: Random House, 1962.

Levy, A., and Merry, U. *Organizational Transformation.* New York: Praeger, 1986.

Morgan, G. *Images of Organization.* Beverly Hills, Calif.: Sage Publications, 1986.

Pfeffer, J. *Organizations and Organization Theory.* Marshfield, Mass.: Pitman, 1982.

JOHN STEWART LEVIN is director of the Community College Institute and associate professor of higher education at the Center for the Study of Higher Education, The University of Arizona.

A participant-observer reconstructs and explains the emergence of the Minnesota State Colleges and Universities system from the merger of three former higher education systems in the state.

In Search of Vision and Values: The Minnesota Higher Education Merger

Steven Wallace

At midnight on July 1, 1995, the highly regarded Minnesota Community College System slipped quietly into history. With it, Minnesota's State University and Technical College systems lapsed into the same statutory nonexistence. In their place emerged the controversial new "megasystem," the Minnesota State Colleges and Universities (MnSCU).

Judith Eaton, the first chancellor of MnSCU, called the new system "the most important experiment in higher education today." It is hard not to be struck by the extremity of the developments in Minnesota, a state once recognized as a leader in progressive, high-quality education. While most businesses in America are pursuing a course of decentralization and demassification, Minnesota chose to create one of the largest educational organizations in higher education history. What may make this "experiment" both important and relevant to community college practitioners across the country is its seductive potential for replication in other states. Accordingly, it is important to consider the implications of the restructuring of higher education in Minnesota.

Whether perceived as an episodic local anomaly or a trend indicator with broad implications, the Minnesota higher education merger provides a substantive and revealing case study relative to the effect of radical higher education policy implemented through legislative mandate. The conditions and tensions that gave rise to this extreme "experiment" are found in part or in whole in many states, if not the majority. Indeed, the combined forces of fiscal limitations, passion for educational reform, and concerns about the efficiency and effectiveness of higher education have in several states resulted in extraordinary legislative responses over which higher educators have had little influence. The large number of merger-related inquiries received by

Minnesota legislators from policymakers in other states indicates the potential for further such developments.

It is reasonable to expect that every state will in some manner reconsider the organization and effectiveness of its higher education system in the near future. This assessment led Minnesota to the arguably valid conclusion that the structure of the state's higher education resources was ripe for improvement as the new global information age began to emerge. It may be true that the traditionally glacial pace of change in institutions of higher education would have been unlikely to produce satisfactory transformation without some form of substantial stimulation. The question in Minnesota, therefore, was not whether to realign higher education with emerging environmental conditions but how to manage public higher education policy in a manner that would improve programs for students constructively and effectively. One often-expressed view was that although merger might represent a viable approach, the form of merger implemented was very wrong for Minnesota. This chapter will address the evolution and the most significant implications of the recent merger of higher education systems in Minnesota.

Historical Background

Minnesota has an interesting history in the development and management of its higher education resources. Community colleges, for example, have been "merged" before. The Minnesota Community College System was formed in 1963 through a last-minute amendment to a bill that afforded oleomargarine the legal authority to be yellow instead of white. Originally developed as the postsecondary extensions of local school districts, the state's twenty-one "junior" colleges were created for the primary purpose of providing lower-division education to university-bound students. Over time, Minnesota community colleges broadened their missions to become the more comprehensive institutions characteristic of their counterparts across the country. The existence of a significant Technical College System limited, however, the full evolution of the career education component on many campuses. Consequently, many community colleges in Minnesota were not able to achieve the desirable balance between liberal arts and technical education programs. Ultimately, one of the most significant processes of the 1995 merger was to address this situation in several ways.

Minnesota's original state universities began as "normal" schools that evolved from teachers' colleges to state colleges to state universities. Traditionally, the seven institutions of the Minnesota State University System were highly autonomous. Shortly before the merger, the system launched an effort to establish a comprehensive urban university serving the populous Minneapolis–St. Paul area without coordination with the other higher education systems. The autonomy and independent style of the state universities made them difficult candidates for merger.

The immediate effect of the higher education merger was the most profound, however, on Minnesota's thirty-five technical colleges. Created by school districts throughout the state, technical colleges began as vocational schools and experienced many title changes before being designated by the legislature as technical "colleges" in 1990. Operating on a noncredit, clock-hour basis without (except in a few cases) accreditation as institutions of higher education, the new colleges struggled with the myriad of challenges attendant on changing a vocational school into a more traditional collegiate form. Long sequences of continuous instruction were broken into discrete courses, credit equivalencies were established, and all technical colleges pursued accreditation through the North Central Association. They remained, however, under the statutory and governance authority of their parent school districts until the effective date of the higher education merger, although many operated joint career programs with neighboring community colleges.

The University of Minnesota, the state's five-campus land-grant university, was not included in the merger because of its autonomy under the state's constitution. Indeed, the inclusion of the University of Minnesota in the higher education merger was not even given serious consideration. As a result, the structure of public higher education in Minnesota changed abruptly from four systems of various sizes with relatively focused missions to two very large multifaceted systems.

The new MnSCU system began on July 1, 1995, with sixty-three colleges and universities, including a university campus in Akita, Japan, and a total enrollment of 156,000 students. The governor appointed a fifteen-member statewide board to operate the new system and formed a new central system office from employees of the three former system offices. Because Minnesota's colleges and universities have never been under the authority of local boards of trustees and have never received direct support from local property taxes, the merger had no effect in these areas.

Why Merge?

The most frequently asked and hotly debated question throughout the introduction and early implementation of the higher education merger was simply, "Why?" Strangely, no clear answer ever emerged. The precipitating cause and attendant vision for the merger must therefore be inferred from its historical antecedents. Factors specific to Minnesota came to interact in the early 1990s with the more universal legislative concerns about higher education's cost, accountability, responsiveness, relevance, and other issues of performance.

For many years prior to merger, Minnesota legislators received periodic complaints from students and parents regarding the transferability of credit between higher education systems. Although objective analysis indicated that the vast majority of actual transfer problems resulted from unaccredited technical colleges, legislators, reacting to the surface value of the complaints, concluded that the problems were caused by the structure of higher education and the unwillingness of the systems to cooperate. Merger, therefore, appeared to be an attractive solution to the "transfer problem." In actuality, transfer practices among accredited colleges and universities were comparatively good. The introduction of the Minnesota Transfer Curriculum in 1994, independent of the merger, made significant further improvements in intersystem transfer. Nonetheless, as perception is reality, legislators continued to react to the anecdotal evidence of a transfer problem. Ultimately, the need to improve transfer became the only substantive cause for merger widely articulated by policy leaders. The identification of transfer as the precipitating cause of reform led many higher educators to conclude that merger was "a dramatic solution to a nonexistent problem."

Another driving force in the interest in merger was concern over a fairly high level of intersystem competition. The competition among different types of institutions was fueled by enrollment-driven funding in the context of diminishing state investment in higher education. As Minnesota decreased its proportion of resources invested in higher education, colleges and universities competed more openly for students. This led some policy leaders to conclude that the structure of higher education was causing inappropriate and wasteful institutional behaviors at a time when the public demanded more collaboration and cost efficiency from the governmental sector.

These and other concerns reached critical mass in 1991 with the introduction of the higher education merger bill in the Minnesota state senate. The bill was authored by the powerful senate majority leader and supported by key senate leaders. Although controversial, the merger bill passed in the senate without significant conceptual compromise. The state house of representatives, however, joined the emphatic opposition from higher educators and students by rejecting the proposed merger. A house/senate conference committee battled over the issue until literally the last minutes of the legislative session. Pressured by a constitutional deadline for adjournment and the senate's credible threat to withhold approval of the omnibus higher education funding bill for the next biennium, the house of representatives grudgingly acceded to the senate position, and the merger of Minnesota's higher education systems became law. Tremendous residual anger among house members regarding both the effects and the process of the merger led to at least three major attempts to repeal the law over the next four years. The senate was successful in defeating each repeal movement, and the merger became effective on July 1, 1995, with no subsequent legislative resistance.

Three characteristics of the success of this sweeping reform initiative are interesting. The first is the absence of any clear precipitating cause; the second, the lack of any substantial constituency other than a very small number of powerful legislators supporting the change; and the third, the virtual absence of any clear vision of how the new system should operate and what outcomes it would be expected to achieve. Combined with the extreme lack of enthusiasm among the newly merged colleges and universities, these conditions presented the leadership of the new MnSCU system with extraordinary challenges.

Ironically, compelling justifications for changes in the structure and operation of higher education existed but were not well articulated. One such rationale for change, for example, lay in the fact that the three large systems operating independently required costly and redundant administrative functions that drew resources away from services to students. Also, very significant and counterproductive funding inequities existed as an undesirable result of long-standing political competition among the systems. In addition, Minnesota's unspoken public policy of disinvestment in higher education had rendered tiny but autonomous institutions, some with enrollment as small as four hundred students (full-time equivalency), financially unsustainable. There was the broader question of how a state with only 4.5 million residents could justify the operation of a sixty-eight–campus public higher education system. Additionally, valid concerns could have been raised about the appropriateness of the three separate systems pursuing independent priorities and agendas in the absence of constructive and concerted direction. These and many other difficult issues led to legitimate interest in structural reform, although not, in the view of many, what actually occurred in Minnesota.

Transition to the Merger

The transition to the merger was an exceedingly traumatic period for Minnesota higher education. Between the passage of the merger law in 1991 and the statutory implementation of the merger in 1995, the new system was expected to form in parallel with the continued operations of the three existing systems. An initial board was formed, and two successive interim chancellors were employed. Very little was accomplished in the first three years of this period, leaving an extraordinarily large and complex body of work to be done in insufficient time just prior to the merger. The second interim chancellor, who served up to the date of the merger, struggled with broad resistance from colleges and universities, the lack of clear legislative intent, and continued efforts to repeal the merger. Students were increasingly vocal in expressing their concerns about the purpose, value, and effects of the merger. The new board experienced not only the usual formative difficulty but also evident divisions of allegiance, as half of the members continued to serve on the boards of the three existing systems. Posters and buttons eventually appeared on campuses asserting, "A billion dollars deserves a plan!,"in reference to the state's biennial subsidy of a new system that appeared directionless.

Governance processes in the new system during the premerger period were difficult. The absence of a clear vision and reasonable performance expectations for the new system resulted in significant ambiguity of purpose and direction. This problem was exacerbated by the nearly universal resistance of those being merged. Tensions reached the boiling point as the second interim chancellor worked unsuccessfully to wrest control from the three existing systems and to implement substantive changes prior to the merger.

One of the most daunting issues of the merger transition was the statutory process of transition itself. According to the law, in a single instant at midnight on July 1, 1995, the Community College, Technical College, and State

University systems were to cease to exist and all authority was to be transferred to the new system. Thus, during the premerger period the new board and system administration had the enormous responsibility of building a massive new organization without any authority over the existing systems. As this situation evolved, it came to look more and more like the transition of Hong Kong from Great Britain to China. Rising tensions were exacerbated toward the end of this period as the interim chancellor demanded the "loan" of increasing numbers of administrators from the three existing systems. The resultant conflicts of accountability and loyalty damaged the operational and organizational effectiveness of all three systems to an increasing extent.

These conditions prevailed on July 1, 1995, when all authority transferred to the new system. Only on the arrival of Judith Eaton, the new system's first continuing chancellor, in mid-August of 1995, did a measure of order and direction begin to emerge. Ultimately, the effectiveness of this initial leader would prove to be a needed corrective in a highly chaotic situation.

Effects of the Merger

The beginning of the new system was marked by significant confusion, conflict, paralysis, and financial distress. Even the naming of the new system was complicated by the fact that people were pronouncing the acronym for the Minnesota State Colleges and Universities as "MISCUE" (hence the lowercase *n* in MnSCU). In private, cynical participants suggested that MnSCU actually stood for "Minnesotans Seeking Chaos and Upheaval." Much of the initial difficulty resulted from partly implemented initiatives from the era of the second interim chancellor and the abrupt, awkward integration of board members, senior administrators, and central office staff from the three former systems. That the new system began with three sets of distinct and often incompatible policies and operating procedures complicated matters. Even more difficult was the existence of three separate sets of former systemwide funding pools subject to dramatically different allocation processes and substantial differences in the level of funding available for similar programs.

Significant problems resulted from the fact that the ownership of all technical colleges transferred from the local school districts to the State of Minnesota, and technical colleges became part of a state agency through their inclusion in the new MnSCU system. As a result, their local labor contracts, facilities agreements, and administrative service arrangements were either invalidated or placed in short-term, interim status.

The biggest difficulty, however, occurred because the legislature refused to provide the funding required to implement the mandate of the merger. Although presented with compelling evidence that a minimum of an additional $60 million was required to integrate the three former systems without significant adverse consequences, the legislature actually reduced funding for the new system. The insufficiency of critically needed resources sharply elevated the levels of stress, protectionism, and organizational dysfunction within the new system.

The politics of the new system became ever more pronounced. Some leaders from the three different types of institutions maneuvered for advantage as the administration and board of the new system struggled to work through a seemingly endless array of diverse and complex issues. Attempts to maintain the segregation of funding streams and attendant variances in allocation levels were among the most prominent activities. Soon, however, the increasing lack of mission differentiation among the three types of institutions became one of the most substantive challenges to the organizational integrity of the new system as technical colleges sought the authority to confer the associate degree and community colleges pursued an interest in the baccalaureate degree.

The most visible early effect of the merger came in the form of institutional consolidations. Many communities in Minnesota had a community college and a technical college in close proximity if not in shared facilities. Following an initiative of the second interim chancellor, the MnSCU board began to consolidate these campuses into single, more comprehensive community and technical colleges. Because the consolidating institutions had dramatically different labor contracts, business practices, policies, and missions, these "minimergers" had a staggering effect on the institutions involved.

Implications of the Merger

Although many characteristics of the Minnesota higher education merger are anomalous and situation-specific, many implications are relevant to community colleges across the country. In the main, these implications derive from omnipresent political considerations, either active or latent, in most parts of the country. In Minnesota these considerations combined to reach critical mass in the form of a radical experiment. In this process, the following forces likely shaped outcomes.

Passion for Reform. The passion for reform is often fueled and legitimized by the corporate view of organizational change held by policy leaders. Intrinsic to this view is the invalid assumption that concepts and methods effective in the restructuring of business entities are equally applicable to institutions of higher education. Accordingly, there is strong commitment to applying successful business models in the quest for education reform. A fatal flaw in this approach, however, is a destructive lack of appreciation for the unique qualities, norms, and protocols of academic organizations and their distinctive cultures. Consequently, the policies of educational reform are susceptible to the misapplication of tools that prove to be entirely ineffective and disruptive in otherwise legitimate efforts to advance the quality of academic institutions.

This phenomenon was strongly evident in the Minnesota higher education merger. Fueled by strong criticism from a few prominent business leaders who perceived a need for reform in education generally, legislators became enamored with merger as a vehicle for higher education reform. Accordingly, easily obtained cost efficiencies and improved executive management were seen as inevitable results of merger.

The most serious consequences of this passion for reform were tendencies to disregard the intense emphasis on human resources and the inherent labor relations complexity in higher education. Not only do Minnesota colleges and universities spend 75 to 80 percent of their resources on compensation, but also their labor contracts are negotiated by powerful unions on a statewide basis. Resulting from an ultimately problematic effort to reduce opposition from organized labor, the merger law guaranteed the continued membership and authority of existing bargaining units. This shortsighted solution did not anticipate the eventual necessity for the structure of bargaining units to evolve to fit the needs of the new merged organization. The result became an increasingly dysfunctional labor environment wherein the most expensive resources of colleges and universities functioned under terms misaligned with important operating requirements.

Seduction of Merger. The passion for radical reform finds easy expression in simplistic solutions such as merger. The decisive and dramatic flair of merger may be seductive to legislators inclined to "drive-by" policymaking. The equivalent of an organizational development sound bite, merger attracts the support of those more interested in achieving big change fast than in dealing with the hundreds of critical issues involved in actually improving organizational effectiveness in the interests of students.

Ambiguity of Vision. Rationality would dictate that a radical organizational change that affects the education of thousands of students and involves the expenditure of hundreds of millions of dollars per year would be grounded in a clear vision of the purposes, advantages, and expected outcomes. Unfortunately, this was not nearly the case in Minnesota. The passion for reform and the seduction of merger as a quick and simple solution eclipsed essential considerations in the formation of the new system. Policymakers in other states may naturally employ a more analytical and visionary approach to the improvement of their higher education resources. They may, however, fail similarly to take the time to become clear on the results they seek and proceed with policy in the absence of a guiding vision.

Misapplication of Business Models. Some Minnesota legislators seemed to be lulled into false complacency by the commonplace nature of mergers and acquisitions in the private sector. The implicit belief seemed to be, "Mergers are done all the time. They are not that big a deal. They seem to work really well." That perception is contradicted, however, by the actual experience of businesses and higher education institutions that have been part of complex mergers. Corporate merger experts who worked with higher education leaders during the implementation of the Minnesota higher education merger indicated that most corporate mergers are highly traumatic and fail to achieve the expected outcomes. They pointed out that none of the key elements in successful mergers—such as clear vision, effective planning, strategic investment, inclusive decision making—were applied in the Minnesota higher education merger, and they expressed concern about what they saw developing in Minnesota.

Significantly, the higher education merger proved to be even more difficult to implement successfully than many corporate mergers. This resulted from the absence of a central organizing principle able to serve as a focal point for integration and organizational development. In the corporate world, the interest in profit provides such a focal point. The nature of higher education institutions, on the contrary, precludes the identification of a central organizing principle that can be easily defined and measured. Even had student achievement become the focal point of a higher education merger, it would have been extraordinarily difficult to define and measure student learning given the enormous programmatic diversity, ranging from vocational diploma programs to the graduate degrees, offered by MnSCU institutions. This diversity militates against the easy integration of organizational elements.

Mythical Savings. The commonly held perception that academic organizations are top-heavy with an excessive number of highly paid administrators may lead policymakers to the questionable belief that cost savings are available through merger. Although eagerly anticipated, this did not prove to be the case in the Minnesota higher education merger. The considerable financial constraints over the several years prior to the merger had already reduced administrative expenditures to minimum levels. Additional cost efficiencies were therefore available only through the abandonment of necessary administrative functions. This was generally not a realistic option. When the expected reduction in administrative personnel did not occur, policy leaders viewed this result as proof of the alleged self-protective tendencies of administrators and evidence of their unwillingness to reduce administrative costs to more reasonable levels.

Other forms of anticipated cost savings failed to materialize as well. Few small programs were closed as a result of the merger, and no campuses were shut down. In fact, the new system quickly adopted a commitment to maintaining all existing campuses to quell accelerating political backlash from concerned rural legislators. The desired economy of scale benefits did not occur due to the geographical dispersion of stand-alone institutions that continued to operate much as they always had.

Ironically, the merger turned out to be a very expensive endeavor. A look at the economic dynamics of corporate mergers would have revealed this almost inevitable effect. Very significant costs were incurred in bringing the technical colleges into state government, reorganizing operations, developing new business practices, and creating new information systems. The governor and many legislators refused, however, to accept these costs as necessary and provided appropriations consistent with the errant premise that a merged organization requires fewer resources. This unwillingness to strategically invest in the success of the merger combined with the great inefficiencies attendant to the implementation of the merger seriously destabilized the new higher education system.

Post-traumatic Shock. Consideration must be given to how the employees of merged institutions will react to and feel about significant and abrupt organizational change. Although the technical act of the merger occurred in a single instant, the resultant traumatic impact was split into two phases arrayed in sequence much like Elizabeth Kubler-Ross's stages of death and dying. Prior to the merger, anticipatory trauma occurred as reactions such as denial and bargaining failed to change the course of the state's new higher education policy. The event of the merger was dominated primarily by feelings and expressions of anger. The most significant phase, however, was the period immediately following the effective date of the merger. In this time, anger transformed rather quickly to grief as the three former systems, in which people were heavily invested, were quickly stripped of their identity, traditions, and long-established practices. A wave of great but relatively pointless nostalgia swept over higher educators as the comfortable and familiar gave way to the chaotic and uncertain.

One of the first victims of the merger was collaboration. Collaboration between higher educators and legislators broke down because of anger and frustration attendant to the early implementation of the merger. Unexpectedly, collaboration among presidents and their institutions began to diminish as collegial groups were abandoned and institutional cooperation devolved to competition as the threatening confusion of the merger began to dominate the environment. A wave of resignations followed as a number of highly regarded education leaders left Minnesota for colleges and universities in other states.

One of the most unfortunate effects of organizational upheaval is the extent to which energy is drawn away from essential purposes to dealing with change. Early in the Minnesota higher education merger, this translated to inattention to student needs and interests. The statewide student associations from the three former systems had opposed the merger from the beginning and became ever more critical as they received little attention in merger planning and implementation. Ironically, students—the putative object of the merger—generally became increasingly alienated. This situation was not addressed until halfway through the second year of the merger, when the new chancellor secured board support for the system's first strategic plan, which carried the theme, "Putting Students First."

Culture Shock. The absence of thorough consideration by legislators of the potential effects of the merger law was also expressed as an insensitivity to the significant cultural differences of the three former systems. Although it was never articulated, the simplistic view that "higher education is higher education" served to mask the difficulties to be encountered with forced integration. Actually, the three systems could hardly have had more different organizational cultures. The technical colleges' origin as the post-secondary vocational extension of high schools had kept them separate from the higher education community. Consequently, traditional collegiate issues such as accreditation, faculty scholarship, course articulation, and general education were not a significant part of their culture. At the other end of the "academic food chain," the state universities had a culture of great autonomy and self-determination. Their interactions with the other two systems had, historically, been in the form of dictating standards for course transfer and upper division admission. As in most universities, lower-division general education and associate degree programs were not a predominating interest. Squarely in the middle, community colleges were, at the point of the merger, already embroiled in a cultural transformation from their original junior college character to becoming more comprehensive institutions. The new and unfamiliar cultural dynamics of the merged system added strain and destabilization to this already difficult process. The most extreme cultural collision, however, occurred in the consolidations of technical and community colleges, which had historically been competitors that had spent years differentiating their missions and organizational cultures.

The culture shock that resulted from forcing these three very different types of institutions together was profound. Expressions of bitter professional dissatisfaction were encountered frequently, particularly among faculty. Many higher education professionals described the first year of the merger as the worst of their career, even when they had personally experienced no significant loss. Their heightened feelings of discontent came, rather, from their negative experiences with cultural changes. Although it is impossible to measure the effect of culture shock on the academic quality of colleges, there is little question that the merger adversely affected teaching, learning, and institutional advancement.

Public Confusion. Public institutions, including college and university systems, have substantial interest in how they are perceived by the public they serve. Dangerously, the constituency most disassociated from and bewildered by the Minnesota higher education merger was the general public. The merger compounded existing confusion regarding the roles and missions of the three former systems. Prior to the merger, the public struggled to understand how increasingly similar community and technical colleges were to be differentiated from a consumer perspective. The programmatic similarity in lower-division general education between community colleges and state universities raised related questions about which students should attend the respective types of institutions. Merging these poorly differentiated (from the public's perspective) systems into a megasystem without a clearly articulated vision resulted in considerable public confusion about the state's strategy for higher education. This confusion was exacerbated as consolidated colleges were given entirely new names, creating the impression that well-known public institutions were disappearing and new colleges of some indeterminate nature were emerging coincidentally. This confusion eroded public support for the merger and resulted in the loss of an opportunity to elevate public enthusiasm for efforts to improve higher education.

Politicization. As all public institutions are creatures of politics, the three former systems had well-established political alliances and agendas. Concern was often expressed before the merger that political competition between the systems was adverse to the educational interests of students. Although the merger itself was a political initiative, there was some hope that the new MnSCU Board would be able to achieve political independence and influence similar to that enjoyed by the University of Minnesota Board of Regents.

Major political issues in the implementation of the merger involved the financial allocation model, the viability of small campuses, and the ability of the MnSCU Board to free itself from the political influences of the former systems and from the narrow political agendas of powerful policymakers. The politics of financial allocation involved the competing interests of highly funded rural colleges seeking to defend their allocation base against the efforts of much less well funded and larger Twin Cities institutions hoping to use the merger as a vehicle for more equitable funding. Altough MnSCU officials initially decided to avoid the issue of equity in funding, the legislature intervened in the system's second biennium through a mandate that effectively froze allocations at current levels. Through this action, the legislature became far more involved in higher education funding policy than was typical before the merger. Similarly, great political pressure from rural legislators protected even the most costly small colleges.

The autonomy of the board became a complicated and controversial issue when, early in the merger, the governor appointed his own chief of staff to the MnSCU Board. A supporter of the merger, the governor had been openly critical of public higher education for many years. The appointment of his chief of staff was therefore perceived to be an aggressive act to secure more political influence over the policies and operations of the new system. Such concerns were significantly heightened a year later when the first chancellor of the new system resigned and the board appointed the governor's chief of staff, who had no higher education experience, as interim chancellor for a period of at least two years. Judith Eaton's departure in less than two years was broadly viewed as a result of excessive politicization of the newly merged system.

Conclusions

Although there are and will continue to be many diverse perspectives on the causes and outcomes of the Minnesota higher education merger, the preponderance of evidence suggests several compelling conclusions. First, no such merger should be attempted without a clearly expressed rationale for dramatic change and a well-articulated vision of what the new form will be and why it will be superior to the old form. A legitimate cause and a clear vision are essential to a successful higher education merger, and the criteria for success and expectations regarding the processes of change should be clearly expressed from the very beginning of merger discussions. Second, the merger of higher education systems must be regarded as an extraordinarily complex process regarding unique and highly sophisticated organizations that are extremely vulnerable to damage from ill-informed and heavy-handed public policy. Careful analysis and planning over a sufficient period of time are necessary to create a new system wherein the whole is more effective than its former parts. Higher education professionals must be allowed to play an appropriate and determinative role in both merger planning and implementation management. Third, higher education mergers must be supported with the investment of sufficient financial resources to ensure effective implementation and eventual success. Where the achievement of immediate cost savings is a driving motivation, an alternative to merger should be pursued. Fourth, all parties to the merger should commit to respecting the distinctive nature of academic institutions and agree to work collaboratively to minimize political interference in the necessary decisions and events of merger. Finally, and most importantly, the interests of students and the improvement of teaching and learning must be maintained as the central focus in every phase and in every decision in the process of merging institutions of higher education.

STEVEN WALLACE is president of Florida Community College at Jacksonville and a former president of Inver Hills, a Minnesota community college.

The 1988 introduction of shared governance into California's community colleges did not ultimately materialize into an anticipated model of collegiality.

Shared Governance in California

Kenneth B. White

In 1988, when the California State legislature enacted AB 1725, a bill designed to modify the contemporary governance structure among the state's 106 community colleges and 71 districts, there was simultaneous rejoicing and consternation. The various constituencies were either convinced that their world was suddenly made whole or that the system had been shamefully and irreparably damaged. It was the introduction of the concept of shared governance into the state's two-year colleges that was at the core of the celebration and the concern (Nussbaum, 1995; Trombley, 1997).

As its architects described it, the aim of shared governance was to bring faculty, many of whom had long felt institutionally disenfranchised, into a stronger position within each college where they would now share authority in specific areas of college activity. What the legislation wrought is something far from its initial goal, something that has raised substantial controversy on most college campuses and at the state chancellor's office in Sacramento (Nussbaum, 1995; Trombley, 1997).

As work on the 1988 legislation evolved, differences emerged over the specific nature of governance reform. State and local board members, in harmony with college administrators, sought application of a traditional approach to "collegiality in higher education" (Nussbaum, 1995, p. 8). State academic senate leaders, however, argued for stronger language. The result was a hybrid with emphasis on a "statutory empowerment model," which went considerably beyond the traditional collegial approach to governance (Nussbaum, 1995; Trombley, 1997).

After nearly a decade, this experiment in legislative engineering is widely viewed as in need of significant repair or reform. Faculty, the one constituency expecting to gain the most, generally find the new governance model unsatisfactory and time consuming, a model that promised much and delivers little.

Students and classified staff, the other elements in the shared governance menage who represent two institutional constituencies relatively new to the intricacies of governance and organizational dynamics, are equally frustrated. Although they were included legislatively, their model for shared governance draws on the collegial and not the bilateral empowerment faculty model (Nussbaum, 1995). Thus, little of a tangible nature has come from the involvement of students and staff. Finally, administrators, implicated as creating the demand for shared governance through what some have characterized as their historically overbearing and autocratic behavior, are equally distraught over the imposition of one more unmanageable mandate from the state capital, Sacramento (Trombley, 1997).

When AB 1725 was under development, those who advocated most vigorously for the bill had at least three goals in view. Shared governance was to create more collegial governance systems, increase the power and influence of local academic senates, and separate community colleges from their K–12 roots by placing them more clearly in a higher education model.

To accomplish these goals, the legislation mandated that colleges and districts work out an agreement to manage academic and professional matters at each institution. Eleven areas were enumerated, and the college administration and governing board working together with each local academic senate were to agree regarding which of these areas their respective constituencies would have primary responsibility over and in which areas the administration would merely collegially consult with the academic senate. Once this was agreed, internal mechanisms were to be established to implement the agreements (California Community Colleges, 1996; Nussbaum, 1995).

If, as many community college educators believe, shared governance has not proven to be an effective governance model, it is reasonable to consider why. Are there factors at the state or local college level that contribute to the broad frustration with the model? Are there, likewise, factors within community colleges from a broader or more systemic perspective that could explain California's two-year college governance dilemma? And, finally, are there elements embedded in this saga that go beyond the two-year college sector and can be explained more readily as reflective of organizational phenomena?

A number of system and institution level factors may have inhibited successful attainment of this state-mandated governance model, including policy implementation or unrealistic assumptions concerning the ability to bring about institutional change through state-level policy adoption, the hybrid character of community college governance and decision making, and the inherent dynamics of both the colleges and the system as fundamentally political organizations.

Policy Implementation

Policy implementation, in this example the adoption and utilization of shared governance at the local college level, has always been an elusive concept. Early theorists were comfortable with the notion that state-level policy adoption led to direct and faithful local implementation. Essentially, this view held that adoption was implementation. In recent years it has become more apparent that policy once adopted may well go through significant modification before it is finally implemented at the institutional or agency level. This belief in adaptive and evolutionary implementation would suggest, for example, that at the institutional level local college employees, or street-level bureaucrats, adapt or modify policy to fit the local context. In a state as diverse and large as California, therefore, the mere adoption of a shared governance policy at the state level will not necessarily yield the desired legislative result at the college level (Bardach, 1977; Berman, 1980; Fullan, 1981; Wildavsky and Majone, 1978).

In practice, each institution has maneuvered and manipulated policy and adapted it to local conditions. The results clearly differ from the original policy intentions, producing myriad unique examples of state policy altered to fit the history and culture of each institution (Nussbaum, 1995).

At Suburban College (a pseudonym of an actual institution), for example, the administration had for decades been viewed by faculty as autocratic, with the president firmly entrenched at the top of the organization. With the mandate for shared governance, the administration delayed and prolonged discussions to such an extent that the faculty largely despaired of ever obtaining meaningful involvement of faculty, staff, and students in college governance, which was the original intent of the legislation. The result at this institution is not a shared governance experience characterized by a collegium but one in which administrators and faculty alike testify that the faculty shares and the administration governs (conversation with the president of the college, August 1996; Nussbaum, 1995).

In the central district office affiliated with Central Community College District, the experience, although quite different, was equally reflective of institutional history and culture. Task forces were immediately created to implement the state policy, resulting in a representative council at each college and one central district shared governance entity. In a district with no history of strong academic senate leadership, the plan moved down a path that, contrary to the goals of AB 1725, anticipated union, not senate, participation in shared governance councils. With some arm-twisting, the senate ultimately gained admission, although the union continues to have a strong role in the shared governance model in this district.

These examples represent but two of the multiple experiences in California's 1725 saga. They reflect not only the challenge of local implementation but also the limitations of legislating policy in a system characterized as a loose confederation of colleges and districts. In California, in spite of increased centralization following the passage of Proposition 13 in 1978, local colleges retain remarkable discretion, not the least of which is the ability to modify state policy at the local implementation stage.

Governance

A case study of two Florida community colleges argues that governance in two-year institutions can be described most accurately as a hybrid of several governance models, and not merely representative of any single model. At times, community colleges behave politically; at times, they behave bureaucratically. They can be simultaneously anarchic and collegial. Thus, it is unreasonably optimistic to believe that a single conceptual approach to governance, in this case the mandate of collegiality, can be grafted successfully onto 1, 10, or 106 community colleges.

Collegial governance, for many both the goal and the result of AB 1725, first emerged in the higher education literature of the 1960s, prompted by the work of John Millett and John Corson (Corson, 1960; Millett, 1962 and 1978). However, this collegial model was quickly challenged by the course of events in the late 1960s and early 1970s. The political upheavals of that era seriously tested the collegial framework. Under these stresses, the flaws inherent in the model became manifest. Collegiality (which looked more and more like a utopian projection than a reflection of reality) was quickly replaced by a political model. The model suggested that colleges were more collections of interest groups engaged in coalition building and other forms of political activity than a community of scholars engaged in shared decision making. Governance and decision making in this conceptualization were seen as a reflection of the power and influence of various coalitions and interest groups within the institution. Conflict was a natural occurrence, and the community of scholars engaging in collegial, consensus decision making quickly receded into the backwater of higher education literature (Baldridge, 1971; Baldridge, Curtis, Ecker, and Riley, 1977).

Political Organizations

Much of the difficulty experienced in California seems to stem from the political nature of all shared governance participants. Time and again, the complaints raised by participants at all levels representing all constituencies categorize their counterparts as guilty of political behavior. Ironically, the very constituent nature of the process itself is rooted in the political governance model. As one recently appointed president remarked, shared governance has become constituency-based decision making for everything from hiring new faculty members to repairing broken pipes. "You have these 'Noah's Ark' committees for everything—two people from this group, two people from that group." The result is "turf battles and gridlock" (Trombley, 1997, p. 9). The diversity of a pluralistic world requires individuals and organizations to reconcile their differences through an acceptable social process. Politics is the means by which unity is achieved out of the diverse and divergent views of the many (Morgan, 1986, p. 142).

Case Study

Two experiences representing two distinct community college districts reflect the core issues associated with the shared governance dilemma in California.

Suburban Community College District is a single-campus, two-year college district. This moderately sized college is, like so many others of the state's two-year colleges, a product of the explosive growth of community colleges in the 1960s. It continues to grow as its service area expands in population and business development. Conversely, Central Community College District is a diverse, two-year, multicollege district with a long and rich history. Unlike its suburban counterpart, Central counts in its ranks one of the oldest colleges in the state. My analysis is based on extensive interviews conducted at these two sites. The colleges named are pseudonyms for actual institutions, and organizational members are referred to only by title.

Suburban Community College entered the shared governance era as its third president was winding down his tenure as CEO. That tenure had been marked by the continuation of a long-established top-down governance and decision-making orientation. Suburban had always been a hierarchical, president-centered institution. Past presidents led autocratically, with leadership styles fluctuating between authoritarian and benevolent dictatorship. These CEOs created an environment that nurtured conflict under the surface of collegiality, and a culture where people generally knew their place. An outward, public emphasis on family masked a dysfunctional college community (conversation with a faculty member, August 1996).

When the state created the regulations necessary to guide implementation of shared governance at the college level, each local institution was expected to develop its own approach to this somewhat elusive concept. At Suburban, the president moved to define the issue and craft an institutional response. The president and the faculty senate appointed members to a collegewide Shared Governance Task Force. This group was charged with extending its efforts to the wider college community through several college working groups. Reports and recommendations were due within twelve to eighteen months. The final goal was the creation of tentative plans for a policy, as well as alternative plans for how the decision-making process might work. Currently, four years later, the college has a new president, board policies related to participation in shared governance by the Academic Senate, the Classified Senate, and the Associated Student Body, but no agreed college-based process for activating the broad state and local policies encouraging shared behavior.

Impediments to the realization of shared governance at Suburban are definitional, historical, and presidential. Definitions of shared governance abound, but there is no consensus across the college on the meaning or intent of the concept. The goals of shared governance are unclear. Although state guidelines attempt to provide clarity, there is little confidence at the college level that state regulations provide the framework for successful implementation. In fact, some believe that the entire concept of shared governance is flawed, a contradiction in terms.

Compounding the absence of goal consensus is the inability of internal constituencies to cooperate. Not only is each constituency suspicious of the motives of the other groups, but also there is a lack of internal cohesion within each group. The faculty, for example, know that a process is absent, yet they cannot articulate a plan that would be appropriate or desirable. The apathy of faculty and staff and their inability to articulate their goals leaves the CEO to design and define the process. The current president appears comfortable with the status quo, which gives him considerable discretion. He eagerly fills the void and cites as one of his most important presidential prerogatives the ability to set the college agenda. This translates into a veto power whereby he can choose to avoid certain items or issues by disconnecting them from the governance process.

Suburban is a prisoner of its history. The president's new administrative team, according to a recent study, is perceived to lack respect for the Suburban culture and its way of resolving problems and making decisions through consultation. Yet there is broad consensus that the culture of the institution as molded by earlier CEOs valued consultation on an individual basis. Favored faculty had access to the president and often obtained support or sanction for individual concerns or initiatives. The result of this was an environment in which, according to the current president, the prevailing concept was one for one and all for none. The introduction of shared governance, even a flawed process, would seem to threaten this prior consultation culture.

In this historical context, conflict at Suburban has generally been low. Only recently, as a result of an ongoing struggle over stalled contract negotiations, has conflict been high and visible. Historically, conflict remained low due to the deal-making nature of the institution and the reluctance of leadership to openly address major issues. In an autocratic environment, public dissent is often ill advised. Since the opportunity existed to solve problems quietly, there was little reason for public displays of hostility or conflict. Even in the arena of shared governance, frustration and concern abound but conflict remains under the surface.

Issues of respect, distrust, betrayal, and communication are persistent in a recent analysis of Suburban. Shared governance is viewed askance by faculty and staff. In this environment, presidential leadership will continue to be challenged. How the president handles these swirling issues will help define his presidential leadership and decision-making ablility. The concluding comment of a recent external analysis might best sum up the issues facing all the players in this drama: "The faculty and staff and administration must assure that they not allow themselves to become captives of a nostalgic notion of the way things were, and thus resist change made necessary by evolving political, social, and economic environments" (from the accreditation report on the college, 1995, p. 24).

Central Community College's shared governance experience reflects both its past and its characteristics as a multicollege institution. Stability would perhaps best describe the culture of the district. Central has had remarkably little change in its leadership over the years. At the district CEO level, two individuals have dominated the position for over twenty years. The governing board prides itself on infrequent turnover among its members, one of whom dates her original tenure to the 1960s. At the presidential level, with two significant recent exceptions, much the same pattern holds true. The same can be said for the staff as a whole. Many faculty members have served for twenty-five years or more, and several mid-level managers have been promoted within from faculty to area deans, to vice presidents, and even to the presidential and district CEO levels.

This continuity seems to have served the district well over many years. Before passage of AB 1725, faculty and staff were content to pursue their interests through the collective bargaining process and work within a loose, but hierarchical, governance structure. As with Suburban, access and problem solving took on a personal rather than a procedural tone.

The emergence of shared governance resulted in dramatic change in the Central Community College District office and at each college. Shared governance processes and procedures quickly became a central issue and were orchestrated through the district CEO at the central office. Task groups were created, and a model quickly emerged that created a council at each college and at the central office. More contentious than the creation of these bodies was the relative roles to be played in them by the faculty union and the college faculty senates. Traditionally strong at Central, the faculty union moved quickly and assertively to maintain its position as the preeminent body representing faculty interests. In a legislative environment where senate power was to become ascendant, the local college senates found themselves struggling to carve out a role in this new world of shared governance. After considerable wrangling, the senates and the union agreed to coexist at both the local college and the district council level.

The experiences in Central Community College District have been multiple and varied. Each college has negotiated its way through the process, and the process has adapted to the college culture. After an initial period of assertiveness on the part of faculty and staff, there has been a general decline in concern over and commitment to shared governance. Institutional life seems to have returned to its pre–AB 1725 equilibrium, as many participants in the process have grown weary and others watching from the sidelines have returned their full attention to teaching and related staff work.

Among all groups, the greatest complaint is the time-consuming nature of this new shared governance arena and its seeming inability to make decisions, at least timely decisions. In Central Community College District there is concern over process at all levels. Although deliberation and discussion have always been a part of the educational arena, there is now a strong sense of drift. Shared governance is seen as contributing to an inability or at least a reluctance to make decisions. Faculty increasingly suggest that shared governance is simply not worth the effort. "Getting anything done," noted one faculty member, "anything, any focus on an issue is extremely difficult. . . . A lot of people simply despair and quit doing it" (conversation with a faculty member, May 1997). According to the former faculty senate president, "[It is] very burdensome, very cumbersome for us. Some welcomed it, some ignored it, some people got burned out early. A majority of faculty aren't happy with shared governance as it is." Asked for a reaction to the possibility that shared governance might never have existed, a longtime faculty leader responded, "I think a whole lot of people would be a lot happier. Some wish it had never happened" (conversations with faculty members, September 1996).

Even at the administrative level, there are serious reservations regarding shared governance. Cynicism at the mid-management and upper management levels abounds. At the highest levels, there is considerable doubt as to any gains derived from the state governance mandate. From this institutional vantage point, the concern becomes external as well as internal. A campus CEO noted, "What would the public say if they knew how much it was costing? Would we lose the public trust if they knew?" (interview with CEO, May 1997).

Such concerns are heightened by administrative interaction with community business leaders. Anxious to forge stronger ties with business and industry, community college administrators are anxious to portray themselves as no-nonsense leaders of very pragmatic institutions. Shared governance does not fit into this self-perception. "I don't know if it [shared governance] is defensible, you know, because all it does is say we're not that much in touch with the real world and I don't think we want them to know that" (interview with administrator, May 1997). At least one CEO likens shared governance to the crazy aunt the family locks in the closet, fearful that the neighbors might find out and think less of them for her affliction.

This disillusionment is reflected in various changes, most notably meeting frequency. At the early stages of shared governance implementation, once councils were established, there was an intense interest in frequent meetings. There seemed to be a sense that failure to meet at least twice monthly could lead to increased administrative prerogative. Quite simply, if faculty and staff were not in almost constant contact with the shared governance mechanism, administrators, sensing a vacuum, would move ahead independently, filling the perceived void without faculty and staff sanction. Presently, councils meet less frequently, once a month at best, and those participating are less committed.

Conclusion

For many college-level participants, shared governance was to be an opportunity for dialogue, discussion, and mutual decision making within a collegium. Here professionals, operating with a sense of mutual respect and a shared vision of the mission and goals of the institution, would decide the short-and long-range direction of these institutions. What they found instead was a model of shared governance that was simultaneously bilateral, legislative, and collegial. As a result of this complex and contradictory model, many local participants have walked away in confusion and frustration, unlikely to return unless and until a new, more satisfactory, model is conceived.

Yet, even had the state adopted a singular and more traditional model, there is little reason to believe that the results would have been significantly different. Here the reason is organizational rather than structural. Colleges operate through a negotiated order, an implicit agreement that allows multiple interests and agendas to coexist within the organization. These groups agree neither on a common mission nor on the distribution of the benefits of institutional membership. Faculty and staff disagree on issues as fundamental as workload, mutual respect, and compensation. Staff and students have different agendas reflecting their unique vantage points within and outside the institution. Certainly, administrators and staff have vastly divergent concerns regarding the day-to-day management of these institutions as well as points of emphasis in setting direction for these colleges.

Here, ultimately, is the rub. These colleges are political, or more specifically pluralistic. Yet not all constituents adopt a pluralistic approach to operations. Consider the experiences of Suburban and Central. Each institution ultimately adhered to the state mandate for shared governance. Each created task groups charged with outlining internal processes for successful implementation of the state policy. At Suburban, the process was stillborn. Faculty and staff expectations for a pluralistic environment were stymied by the unitary reality of its autocratic administrative culture. Suburban continues to be without a meaningful process that includes each of the institution's constituent groups.

At Central, the process differed but the results appear to be the same. The district used a seemingly open and inclusive system to arrive at multiple mechanisms for shared governance, creating a model that included senates, unions, and students. After less than a decade, the participants are weary and disillusioned. The process, heralded across the state by district leaders only a few years ago, seems ready to fall into disuse.

Shared governance at these institutions is a hollow version of what many anticipated in 1988 when the legislature enacted AB 1725. The adoption of a complex state model and the failure to address the complexities of organizational life in local institutions presaged this unhappy and unfortunate outcome. Any remedy lies in the ability of state and local leaders to recognize and address these structural and organizational variables.

Recommendations

Ironically, this shared governance dilemma is not the sole province of the two-year sector. Four-year institutions are also bemoaning the decline of the fundamental principles of shared governance. Citing everything from faculty apathy to the intrusion of corporate culture, these institutions are concerned that shared governance is following the dinosaurs into eventual extinction.

What each sector has in common is the fundamental need to address this problem at the local level. Each institution exists in its own unique political environment and contains its own set of historic and cultural variables. To forge a successful shared governance relationship, institutions must accept both their past and their present.

Each institution must be willing to consider unique options that address the substance of their experience, history, and culture. All participants must endeavor to suspend their inherent view of the situation and be open to new, untested, and potentially dangerous options. This will require creative thinking on the part of all parties. It may, in fact, require that administrators yield some of their control and that faculty accept a greater share of the responsibility, even the legal responsibility, for decisions made in a joint enterprise.

Finally, as local college personnel review their unique circumstances and devise individualized solutions, they would do well to consider the role of students and staff in the shared governance process. To this point it has been folly to assume that faculty, staff, students, and administrators participate equally and simultaneously in the shared governance environment. Students in a community college are overwhelmingly part-time. The vast majority have neither the time nor the inclination to participate in the decision making of shared governance. To pretend that they are participants only adds to the futility and the absurdity of the current governance system. Staff also have not been equal participants. The staff at many two-year colleges have historically been treated as second-class citizens. In a system dominated by administrators and faculty, it is almost cruel to imply that staff will share in the process when neither of the other two sides anticipates full and equal participation. It might be better to leave them out of the equation than to continue to act out a farce.

It has been a decade since the passage of AB 1725, and the debate and discussion over shared governance have not abated. This year's annual senate retreat at Central Community College District focused on shared governance. Both 1998 CEO retreats in the state have the issue high on their respective agendas, and the chancellor's office maintains it as an exceedingly high priority. If shared governance is to move out of the netherworld of mythology and into reality, it will require perceptive and local efforts by faculty and administrators alike.

References

Baldridge, J. V. *Power and Conflict in the University.* New York: John Wiley, 1971.

Baldridge, J., Curtis, D. V., Ecker, G. P., and Riley, G. L. "Alternative Models of Governance in Higher Education." In G. C. Riley and J. V. Baldridge (eds.), *Governing Academic Organizations.* Berkeley: McCutcheon, 1977.

Bardach, E. *The Implementation Game: What Happens After a Bill Becomes Law.* Cambridge, Mass.: MIT Press, 1977.

Berman, P. "Thinking About Programmed and Adaptive Implementation: Matching Strategies to Situations." In H. M. Ingram and D. Mann (eds.), *Why Policies Succeed or Fail.* Beverly Hills, Calif.: Sage Publications, 1980.

California Community Colleges. *Developing a Model for Effective Senate/Union Relations.* Sacramento: California Community Colleges, 1996. (ED 395 628)

Corson, J. J. *Governance of Colleges and Universities.* New York: McGraw-Hill, 1960.

Fullan, M. "Research on the Implementation of Educational Change." In A. C. Kerckhoff (ed.), *Research in Sociology of Education and Socialization.* Vol. 2. Greenwich, Conn.: JAI Press, 1981.

Millett, J. D. *The Academic Community.* San Francisco: McGraw-Hill, 1962.

Millett, J. D. *New Structures of Campus Power.* San Francisco: Jossey-Bass, 1978.

Morgan, G. *Images of Organizations.* Beverly Hills, Calif.: Sage Publications, 1986.

Nussbaum, T. J. *Evolving Community College Shared Governance to Better Serve the Public Interest.* Sacramento: California Community Colleges, 1995. (ED 397 922)

Trombley, W. "Shared Governance: An Elusive Goal." *Crosstalk,* 1997, 5 (1), 7–14.

Wildavsky, A., and Majone, G. "Implementation as Evolution." In H. E. Freeman (ed.), *Policy Studies Review Annual,* Vol. 2. Beverly Hills, Calif.: Sage Publications, 1978.

KENNETH B. WHITE *is currently professor of history at Modesto Junior College, California, and is former president of Columbia College in California.*

The Puente Project is offered as an exemplar of academic and cultural approaches that welcome and socialize Latino students to college while increasing their self-esteem, persistence, academic success, and transfer rates.

An Organizational Response to Welcoming Students of Color

Berta Vigil Laden

More than any other institutions of higher education, community colleges play a pivotal role in educating students from diverse racial and ethnic backgrounds. As the largest single sector, consisting of more than one-third of all higher education institutions, community colleges educate over five million students annually (Pincus and DeCamp, 1989) and nearly half of all students of color (Carter and Wilson, 1996). Moreover, community colleges continue to attract students of color at a higher rate than four-year institutions. For example, from 1988 to 1992, a 35.5 percent enrollment increase occurred in two-year colleges, compared to a 28.7 percent increase in four-year colleges (Carter and Wilson, 1994). With the trend of public colleges and universities to eliminate race and ethnicity as factors in their selective admissions process, the number of students of color selecting community colleges is expected to continue to rise (Carter and Wilson, 1996).

As Rendón and Garza (1995) remind us, Latinos and Native Americans, and to a large extent African Americans, tend to choose the path of the community colleges out of necessity if they want any college education at all. As well, these students often use community colleges as the higher educational entry point to transfer to senior institutions if they want to pursue a baccalaureate or higher degree (Laden, 1994).

Several organizational questions arise as a result of the increasing number of students of color who continue to choose the community colleges as a point of entry. How have community colleges responded to students of color to foster higher retention rates and academic success for them? What socialization practices are enacted by the organization to promote the development and refinement of attitudes and abilities that members of color, particularly Latino students, bring to the community college?

NEW DIRECTIONS FOR COMMUNITY COLLEGES no. 102, Summer 1998 © Jossey-Bass Publishers

In this chapter, I use the example of the Puente Project, a California community colleges and University of California partnership for Latino transfer students, to illustrate a positive organizational response to one group of students underrepresented in the aggregate in higher education. The data collection methods used include semistructured interviews with administrators, faculty, and Puente Project staff at two community colleges, telephone interviews with Puente Project staff at the state level, and a review of the research literature, reports, newsletters, newspapers, and other archival data pertaining to the Puente Project and the Latino undergraduate experiences.

Organizational Responses to Students of Color

Issues of cultural diversity have had an effect on community colleges since the 1960s, when students of color began to enroll in record numbers in what were referred to then as open-door colleges (Clark, 1960) or democracy's colleges (Brint and Karabel, 1989). For over thirty years organizational responses have varied from systemic to individual institutional approaches in managing the welcoming and incorporating of students of color into the academic and social processes of the institution. Depending on the geographical locations of community colleges, the demographics of students of color have varied and thus influenced the types and variety of programmatic offerings. Some of these offerings are offset by federal and state categorical funds. For example, among the federal and state programs, TRIO, EOPS, and Title III programs assist low-income and ethnically diverse community college students who are the first in their families to attend college.

Organizational changes have occurred in other ways, as well. Beginning in the mid 1980s, state reform movements to increase both associate degree completion rates and transfer rates to four-year colleges and universities, especially for low-income and underrepresented minority students, also led to a number of changes, such as the development of transfer centers in the community colleges. The creation of transfer centers also led to an increased outreach role by four-year institutions into community colleges and an improvement of course and program articulation agreements between these institutions to raise transfer rates. A number of new programs dedicated to assist students of color to persist and to complete their academic goals of transferring or graduating also flourished. Among the most successful have been programs that take into account the students' socioeconomic and cultural backgrounds (Laden, 1994).

According to some researchers (Laden,1998; Rhoads and Valadez, 1996; Tierney, 1997; Van Maanen, 1984), Latinos and students of color in general bring critical cultural knowledge and values with them to the community college that educators can use to influence these students' motivation and academic achievement by acknowledging and further enhancing the cultural contexts that form part of their identities. More specifically, students can learn the new organizational culture they now inhabit while college administrators and faculty can simultaneously facilitate and support students' entry through celebratory activities. These activities welcome and consider students' diverse experiences and multiple ways of gaining knowledge and understanding.

The Role of Culture and Organizational Socialization

Central to examining an organization and its efforts to address the needs of its members, be they newcomers or long-time members, are the culture and the socialization practices present. Every organization has an embedded culture, and newcomers are socialized to the norms, values, and behaviors of that organization, whether harshly and intensively or benignly and supportively (Van Maanen, 1984). Tierney (1997) advocates considering the nature of the organizational culture in which newcomers are socialized by examining the organizational process individuals use to gain new knowledge, skills, and dispositions expected to make them effective members of society.

Certainly, organizational socialization of newcomers occurs in every organization and social setting, but how is it defined? According to Van Maanen, organizational socialization is defined as a "theory about how new skills, belief systems, patterns of action and, occasionally, personal identities are acquired (or not acquired) by people as they move into new social settings" (1984, p. 211). Moreover, Van Maanen notes two contrasting forms of organizational socialization that newcomers to an organization may undergo. The more traditional organizational form expects newcomers to enter the particular social setting with the intent to conform their conduct to an image of what is desirable and proper organizationally, thus leading to a process that systematically reduces whatever diversity exists among the newcomers at entry. Tierney views this form from a modernist perspective in which the socialization is a "process where people 'acquire' knowledge, [through] a one-way process in which the initiate learns how the organization works, and the socialization is a little more than a series of planned learning activities" (1997, p. 5). In other words, newcomers are socialized to fit into a specific homogeneous culture where individuals are expected to sublimate or shed their own cultural attitudes and behaviors and learn to act in certain already established cultural ways congruent with other members' attributes and behaviors in the organization.

On the other hand, the less traditional form of organizational socialization takes advantage of whatever attitudes and skills newcomers already possess, while members of the organization do what is possible to encourage the newcomers to exhibit and further refine such attributes. Van Maanen refers to this form of socialization as a "celebratory socialization" because it offers welcoming and confirming ceremonies that ease the transition of newcomers to the new setting and builds on preserving their heterogeneity. From the postmodernist perspective, Tierney states that culture is not "waiting 'out there' to be discovered and 'acquired' by new members . . . [but rather] the organization's culture derives from the partial and mutually dependent knowledge of each person caught in the process and develops out of the work they do together" (1997, p. 6). Thus, Tierney refers to this type of socialization as a give-and-take process that allows newcomers to make sense of the organization by using their own unique cultural backgrounds and contexts. Individuals are expected not to put aside their own attributes and behaviors but rather to blend their own with those of the current organizational culture to create an ever more distinctive culture that welcomes and celebrates the contributions of all participants.

In examining the Puente Project, I apply the concept of celebratory socialization to highlight how the cultural background of the students is embraced as the keystone of various higher education organizational components of the Puente Project. Moreover, I hold with the concept advocated by others (Rhoads and Valadez, 1996; Tierney and Rhoads, 1991) that the celebratory and dynamic process is a bidirectional socialization that occurs in the organizational culture and transforms both the newcomers and the long-term members of the organization through contact with each other. That is, as newcomers enter the organization, their dynamic interactions with other members lead to changes not only in the newcomers themselves but also in other members of the organization, thus transforming the organization itself by their presence.

How newcomers are welcomed and socialized into an organization is particularly important for students of color. It is not uncommon for students of color to juggle two cultures in college—their own distinctive culture and that of the college, with the student's own culture more typically subordinated to the dominant culture of the organization. Student involvement and persistence to graduation become problematic for those who feel particularly unwelcomed in the new environment. In fact, for most students of color their most serious concern is not college admission but dealing with the problems they confront once they are matriculated. These problems span a range. They include the anxiety of breaking close family ties, loneliness and tensions inherent in finding their way around an alien culture, and coping with courses they are not necessarily well prepared for, given that many students of color come from poorer, less academically stringent high schools. Also, a less visible but considerable problem is the one of dealing with the subtle and not-so-subtle discrimination built around the concept of being a minority student who is perceived to have received special treatment in college admissions while other more qualified (that is, white) students were kept out (Fiske, 1988; Zwerling and London, 1992). All of these factors often lead to a severe case of culture shock for many of these students, who are thrown on their own into a new organization with no one to offer a distinctive cultural welcoming into the unknown but seemingly homogenous world of the dominant group.

In this light, the concept of celebratory socialization (Tierney, 1997; Van Maanen, 1984) highlights a process that attempts to break down the confusion and alleviate culture shock by welcoming students and instilling a sense of belonging to the organization from the very beginning. Inherent in this process is the valuing of the students' cultures and recognizing their distinctiveness while building on their socialization experiences and knowledge acquisition through culturally appropriate academic and student support programs. Rhoads and Valadez expand the concept of celebratory socialization to support the multiple forms of knowledge and ways of understanding that diverse members bring with them to college. They further assert that celebratory socialization processes support a multicultural mission by embracing border knowledge, "knowledge that resides outside the canon, outside of the cultural mainstream" (1996, p. 7), such as that border knowledge that students of color and their cultural contexts bring to the college setting and that often remains unacknowledged or invalidated.

A Model Organizational Response to Specific Students of Color

Of particular concern for California policy makers and educators are the low transfer rates and enrollment of Latinos in the California public four-year colleges and universities. To address these imbalances, a number of organizational, programmatic efforts to overcome barriers and build bridges between the two-and four-year systems leading to greater academic success rates for Latinos have been undertaken. Among those of highly notable success is the Puente Project, targeting Latino students in their first year of community college. Operating out of the University of California Office of the President, the Puente Project works with thirty-eight institutions, slightly more than one-third of the 106 community colleges in the state.

The Puente Project was initially conceived in 1981 as an internal organizational response to address the perceived needs of Latino community college students at Chabot College, located in the San Francisco bay area (McGrath and Galaviz, 1996a). Concerned about the high dropout rate for Latinos at Chabot College, Patricia McGrath, an English faculty member, and Felix Galaviz, a counselor and assistant dean, undertook a thorough examination of over two thousand transcripts of Latino students. McGrath and Galaviz discovered that these students were not following a logical sequence of courses leading to specific majors, often ignored prerequisites, took very few general education courses necessary to meet either associate degree or transfer requirements, and had little to no contact with academic counselors. Moreover, Latino students were disproportionately enrolled in remedial writing courses. There was also little movement into advanced English classes, which provide opportunities to develop reading and writing skills necessary for transfer. The review of transcripts also suggested that in all likelihood most of these students were first-generation college students; thus, they probably had no family members to provide informal academic guidance or orientation to college.

With these data in mind, McGrath and Galaviz designed a program of linkages to help Latinos persist in college and succeed academically, transfer to senior institutions to earn their bachelor's and advanced degrees, and return to their communities as leaders and mentors. McGrath and Galaviz named the program the Puente Project, using the Spanish word *puente,* meaning bridge, as its symbolic keystone for conveying the concept of building bridges institutionally, inter-institutionally with four-year colleges, and with the greater community. Of special emphasis in the Puente Project are the threefold goals of (1) two semesters of intensive English instruction focusing on writing and reading about the students' Latino cultural experiences and identity; (2) Latino counselors who have first-hand knowledge of the challenges that students face; and (3) mentors from the Latino professional and academic community (McGrath and Galaviz, 1996b).

Moreover, from the very beginning, the role of the Latino community, offering both external and internal organizational underpinnings, was seen by McGrath and Galaviz as crucial, and having the greatest stake in the success or failure of the education of all its Latino youths. McGrath and Galaviz (1996a) reasoned that greater involvement by all segments of the Latino community leads to greater institutional accountability and responsiveness, and ultimately to a more effective educational environment. With these various goals in mind, they launched the Puente Project as a practical, cost-effective model for Latino students that would address their unique needs through sensitivity to and affirmation of their ethnic identity by building on their cultural strengths (McGrath and Galaviz, 1996b), much along the lines of the celebratory socialization advocated by some researchers (Laden, 1998; Rhoads and Valadez, 1996; Tierney, 1997; Van Maanen, 1984). In effect, the students' border knowledge was validated and incorporated into the curriculum rather than ignored or dismissed.

Puentistas Connect an Academic Program with a Cultural Context

The term *Puentistas* quickly emerged in the lexicon of the Puente Project participants. The Spanish word *puentista* can be broadly interpreted to mean a person who is crossing a bridge or a person who builds bridges. Central to the concept of the Puente Project is the connection between the cultural context of the students and the academic environment of the Puente program and the larger organization as a whole. Consequently, at least one of the two Puente faculty participants must be a Latino. Moreover, the faculty begin their own bridge crossing by participating in an intensive summer training course held at UC Berkeley each summer for new Puente faculty. Among the activities, the faculty do the same curricular exercises the student *Puentistas* will do during the academic year.

Specifically, the Puente Project cultural model offers a tri-bridge approach that leads to successful academic outcomes, increased self-esteem, and greater self-confidence for Latino students. The fundamental bridges that welcome *Puentistas* into the program and help them move toward academic success in college are the three bridging components of writing, counseling, and mentoring.

The writing component of the project is based on a two-course sequence of accelerated writing instruction. A cohort of thirty first-year students enrolls in a pretransfer developmental English course in the first term and in a transfer-level English composition class in the second term with the same Puente faculty. Puentistas begin by reading Latino literature and writing compositions based on their culture and community, drawing from their own life experiences, their families and friends, their neighborhoods, and all that is most intimately familiar to them. In the second term oral and written exercises in the classroom are incorporated based on activities with their mentors and guest Latino writers and artists who emphasize ways to remain true to their own cultural identities while achieving success in the mainstream society.

The academic counseling component provides daily contact between the counselor and the students. The counselor offers typical academic and career guidance and information, such as information about degree and transfer requirements, financial aid, and the college application process, along with personal encouragement, motivation, and psychological support to persist and succeed in what for many is still an alien environment. Other commitments include outreach efforts for new students, selecting and training mentors as well as pairing them with students, and working closely with parents to help them to understand and become involved with their children's college experiences.

The mentoring component relies on volunteers from the Latino professional and academic communities who receive training and commit to spending at least sixteen hours per year with their mentees. The mentors invite mentees to their work sites and professional meetings, attend specific class and off-campus activities, and interact with them personally, thus generally sharing their professional and personal lives with them. Central to the mentoring relationship is the notion that as successful Latino professionals, the mentors are able to retain their cultural identity while achieving their academic and career goals (McGrath and Galaviz, 1996b).

The tri-partite approach of the Puente program produced results in the first year that far exceeded McGrath and Galaviz's expectations. For example, the students' overall grade point average rose from 1.64 prior to Puente to 2.70 after two semesters in the program, even though these students were enrolled in three times as many academic courses as they had been before their entry into the Puente Project. Moreover, a 100 percent persistence rate was achieved, with the return of all the students the following academic year (McGrath and Galaviz, 1996b). Additionally, of the pilot Puentista cohort, 33 percent transferred to a senior institution, compared to the fewer than 5 percent of all Latino community college students transferring at that time (UC Office of the President, 1992).

In 1985, the success of the Puente Project led to a partnership between the California community colleges and the University of California. The UC Office of the President provides administrative and fiscal oversight and office space for the Puente Project staff while the California community colleges chancellor's office coordinates efforts among the community colleges that participate in the partnership (University of California, 1993). McGrath and

Galaviz continue their affiliation with the Puente Project by serving as its codirectors. As a partner, the University of California provides summer and midyear training for faculty, hosts special Puente transfer conferences each fall and spring at various UC campuses, and funds other related programmatic and outreach activities.

The empirical data continue to reveal positive results of the Puente Project, according to the UC Office of the President. While each of the thirty-eight community colleges involved enrolls approximately thirty Puente students a year, thus serving approximately 1,200 new students annually, another 1,800 continuing students are served annually with an astounding 97 percent retention rate and a 95 percent involvement of the Puentista parents in Puente activities as well. At least 48 percent of all students who complete the Puente program transfer to a four-year institution. Of these, 30 percent enroll in one of the nine UC campuses, compared to 22 percent of all community college transfer students to UC. Another 56 percent of Puente transfer students enroll in one of the twenty-two California state universities (Stough, 1996). Although empirical data continue to be gathered and analyzed, preliminary evidence suggests that an increasing number of Puentistas are enrolling in graduate school after receiving their bachelor's degrees (Rouleau, 1997).

Discussion

The Puente Project provides a model for how an educational organization can incorporate and share the cultural mosaic of U.S. society in new, interesting, and successful ways. By inviting Latino students into the community college, the Puente Project provides a web of connections and caring communities as suggested by Gilligan (1982) and Mittelstet (1994) that not only incorporate but celebrate the cultural identities of its diverse populations. The organizational structure of the Puente Project has enabled partnerships to develop among community colleges, universities, and the business and professional sectors in California. The intent of the project is to welcome Latino students through tri-partite celebratory, socializing processes that offer pedagogical and transformative experiences that reach beyond the students themselves. Results indicate that the Puente Project helps students raise their educational and career aspirations, achieve their academic goals, and increase both their self-esteem and their self-confidence. These are accomplished by students with a sense of personal and cultural pride in remaining true to who they are while exploring and developing in new directions in the world of higher education.

The organizations involved also have changed in their policies and practices as a result of interactions with individuals who are part of the Puente Project. For example:

- Faculty participants in the Puente Project take their new expertise into their other classes; non-Puente faculty have the opportunity to see the positive outcomes of the program on Latino students.

- Administrators are more supportive, given the encouraging results of the program.
- Inclusion of people from the greater Latino community as mentors, parents, and guest speakers supports the cultural, celebratory underpinnings of organizational socialization.
- The extended role of the University of California signifies a large commitment of resources to community colleges and Latino students in particular.
- Institutional linkages are created among community colleges, the university system, and the business community.

The Puente Project template for increasing the retention and academic achievement of Latino students at educational institutions can be emulated to assist underrepresented and low-socioeconomic-level student groups, or any non-majority students who may feel marginalized. Some questions arise about the program, nonetheless. How can the Puente Project be modified to broaden the concept of celebratory socialization to more students? How does a program such as this, serving a specific ethnic population, address affirmative action concerns?

Several aspects of the model have already been modified by some community colleges. One modification is the inclusion of more courses in addition to English. A community college in northern California offers a program modeled on the Puente Project that incorporates mathematics courses along with English. A college in southern California includes a range of ten general education courses and a summer bridge program with basic reading, writing, and mathematics review courses to help the students obtain a head start in college. A wider array of course offerings has the added advantage of involving more college personnel in the reciprocal process of organizational socialization, thus moving the organization as a whole toward greater understanding of the individual members within it.

Other changes include the provision of greater access by opening up the program to more students each semester rather than having them wait until the fall of each academic year to join a new cohort. In addition, the Puente Project is currently offered only to day students; hence the opportunity exists to offer the program to evening students, who often attend in greater numbers than day students in many community colleges (Laden, 1994). Greater access also includes inviting other underrepresented student groups who are under-enrolled in college. The heart of the Puente Project—the tri-partite components that welcome and help students to become members of the collegiate organizational setting—can incorporate all students who currently do not fit into a mainstream organizational model of socialization.

Although participation in the Puente Project is now open to all interested students (Rouleau, 1997), the program primarily attracts Latinos in light of courses designed specifically for them. Potentially, affirmative action concerns may surface in that matriculated non-Latino students who are not familiar with Spanish can challenge the use of curricular content offered in Spanish, even if translations or bilingual versions are available.

Implications

The Puente Project offers policy makers and practitioners a model that lends itself to modification for other student groups. The ability to involve the greater community, namely the parents and Latino professionals, is one of the benefits of this program that should be attractive to educational decision makers as well. Furthermore, rather than treating programs such as the Puente Project as discrete entities within one institution or one system, these programs offer the opportunity to create and maintain an extended, integrated educational pipeline among state and local community colleges, high schools, and four-year colleges and universities to facilitate the retention and academic success of Latinos and students of other racial or ethnic groups who are underrepresented in higher education. Already the concept is undergoing pilot testing in some high schools in California. The model has potential to be adapted in undergraduate and graduate programs as well.

Moreover, the concept of celebratory socialization highlights how educational institutions and their members can create bridges to reach out to all their students, to the larger community, and to the expanded kindergarten-through-graduate educational continuum to reach a greater number of racially and ethnically diverse individuals and help them move further along the educational pipeline. The organizational practices that embrace and validate the cultural differences of students also have the effect of shaping the organization itself and thus reshaping organizational culture. The Puente Project provides a model that can be emulated throughout education, from kindergarten to graduate school, and the approach is not restricted to one cultural group or one population. The concept of celebratory socialization can be embedded in any organization that is open to new challenges and changes.

References

Brint, S., and Karabel, J.. *The Diverted Dream: Community Colleges and the Promise of Educational Opportunity in America, 1900–1985.* New York: Oxford University Press, 1989.

Carter, D., and Wilson, R. *Annual Status Report on Minorities in Higher Education.* Washington, D.C.: American Council on Education, 1994.

Carter, D., and Wilson, R. *Annual Status Report on Minorities in Higher Education.* Washington, D.C.: American Council on Education, 1996.

Clark, B. "The Cooling Out Function in Higher Education." *American Journal of Sociology,* 1960, 65 (6), 569–576.

Fiske E. B. "The Undergraduate Hispanic Experience." *Change,* May–June 1988, pp. 29–33.

Gilligan, C. *In a Different Voice.* Boston: Harvard University Press, 1982.

Laden, B. V. "The Educational Pipeline: Organizational and Protective Factors Influencing the Academic Progress of Hispanic Community College Students with Potential at Risk Characteristics." Unpublished Ph.D. dissertation. Palo Alto, Calif.: Stanford University, 1994.

Laden, B. V. "Empowering Culturally Diverse Students Through Celebratory Socialization in Academic Programs and Support Services." In K. Shaw, J. Valadez, and R. Rhoads (eds.), *Community Colleges as Cultural Texts: Ethnographic Exploration of Organizational Culture.* New York: State University of New York Press, 1998.

McGrath, P., and Galaviz, F. "The Puente Project." *On Common Ground: Strengthening Teaching Through School-University Partnership* (Yale–New Haven Teachers Institute, Yale University), fall 1996a, p. 7.

McGrath, P., and Galaviz, F. "In Practice: The Puente Project." *About Campus,* 1996b, *1* (5), 27–30.

Mittelstet, S. K. "A Synthesis of the Literature on Understanding the New Vision for Community College Culture: The Concept of Community Building." In G. A. Baker III (ed.), *A Handbook on the Community College in America.* Westport, Conn.: Greenwood Press, 1994.

Pincus, F. L., and DeCamp, S. "Minority Community College Students Who Transfer to Four-Year Colleges: A Study of a Matched Sample of B.A. Recipients and Nonrecipients." *Community/Junior College,* 1989, *13* (s3–4), 191–219.

Rendón, L. I., and Garza, H. "Closing the Gap Between Two-and Four-Year Institutions." In L. I. Rendón, R. O. Hope, and Associates, *Educating a New Majority: Transforming America's Educational System for Diversity.* San Francisco: Jossey-Bass, 1995.

Rhoads, R. A., and Valadez, J. R. *Democracy, Multiculturalism, and the Community College: A Critical Perspective.* New York: Garland Publishing, 1996.

Rouleau, J. A. "Conversation with Joan Rouleau, Puente Project Public Information Officer." Oakland: University of California Office of the President, 1997.

Stough, J. "Puente by the Numbers." *Puente News* (University of California at Oakland), fall 1996, p. 4.

Tierney, W. G. "Organizational Socialization in Higher Education." *Journal of Higher Education,* 1997, *68* (1), 1–16.

Tierney, W. G., and Rhoads, R. A. "Postmodernism and Critical Theory in Higher Education: Implications for Research and Practice. In J. C. Smart (ed.), *Higher Education: Handbook of Theory and Research.* New York: Agathon, 1991.

University of California. *Latino Student Eligibility and Participation in the University of California: Report Number Two of the Latino Eligibility Task Force.* Santa Cruz: University of California, 1993.

University of California Office of the President. *Puente: Creating Leaders.* Oakland: University of California Office of the President, 1992.

Van Maanen, J. "Doing New Things in Old Ways: The Chains of Socialization." In J. L. Bess (ed.), *College and University Organization: Insights from the Behavioral Sciences.* New York: New York University Press, 1984.

Zwerling, S. L., and London, H. B., (eds.). *First-Generation Students: Confronting the Cultural Issues.* New Directions for Community Colleges, no. 80. San Francisco: Jossey-Bass, 1992.

BERTA VIGIL LADEN *is assistant professor at Vanderbilt University, Tennessee.*

Whereas some organizational members describe change as externally generated, others are convinced that change is internally planned. In this examination of community colleges, actions of organizations are conceived of as the interplay between external and internal forces.

Making Sense of Organizational Change

John Stewart Levin

At College 1, if you talk to the college president or the district chancellor, you have the sense that a revolution in education is under way. The district chancellor gesticulates, pointing the way to the future and explaining that the college is addressing the needs of new learners, those no longer interested in traditional content or traditional pedagogical methods. They want to be able to cope and succeed in the global environment. The president of the college displays the diagram of the new structure of the college: organized not by departments or divisions but by communities, to model the customer and the customer's needs. There is no longer a visual image of school or college or academic departments here; instead the model is one of thematic organization, such as "Multicultural Studies," "Personal Success,"and "Human Needs." These replace the units formerly called "Arts and Sciences," "Student Services," and "Human Resources." Both chancellor and president, as well as several senior managers, suggest that these alterations arise from college responsiveness to external conditions and college strategy to maintain a leadership role among community colleges nationwide. But there is a noticeable institutional disjuncture over this image.

First, faculty and other administrators portray a different image of the institution. This image is largely political in its emphasis, characterized by faculty and administration separateness, union and management conflicts, and friction among groups in the college over the mission of the institution.

This chapter is based on a research investigation funded by the Social Sciences and Humanities Research Council (Canada).

43

Second, faculty and several administrators attribute change not to college responsiveness to the external environment but to the college leadership's motivation to maintain a specific image of the institution. David, in the Biology Department, suggests that the college is trapped in its own rhetoric of an innovative institution and that its buildings, its equipment, and its institutional spirit for improvement have deteriorated. An administrative colleague of David's says that the faculty will not compromise on quality and that they will neither change their teaching approaches nor embrace new technologies. Another administrator harkens back to the past of the college, when productivity was high and interpersonal relations were foremost. Fear has replaced collegiality, fear about losing jobs in the face of new management priorities and practices.

Unlike the college president and district chancellor, these college members have little to say about the external environment: they are fully occupied with the internal college. Change for them is what has been lost from the past, and they are just as fervent about their image of the past and its qualities as the president and chancellor are about the future.

At College 2, the college president reads from the college's revised mission statement to underline the college's intentions to emphasize its local orientation: to meet the needs of ordinary adult community members for basic education, skill and job training, and career preparation. He cites evidence of declining government financial support, new populations in need of specialized training, and a more highly competitive and global marketplace as the forces acting on the college. A long-serving faculty member who performs an administrative role at the college explains that the institution is outdated technologically and programmatically and has become an adult training institution. "There is no choice here," he claims, "Our faculty and our administrators are living in the nineteenth century, a bunch of Luddites." A group of administrators at the college indicate that their time is consumed with meetings, largely with other administrators, that they have "no time for their work," and that they are unsure of what or whom they are managing. The disjuncture here is about perceptions among organizational members and about what gives rise to institutional change.

Introduction

Organizational change in the community college is conveyed by storytelling: through descriptions and explanations that organizational members give to make sense not only of their organization but also of the relationship between the organization and its environment. This chapter examines the descriptions and explanations of organizational members in community colleges that portray change in the institution and identify sources and precipitators of change.

Members and external stakeholders of organizations endeavor to make sense of organizational actions and events: they tell stories that either explain these phenomena or fit into an existing framework of understanding (Astley,

1985). How and why organizations change are conundrums of organizational theory. Foremost among these conundrums is the tension that exists between external determination and internal direction of change (Pfeffer, 1982).

On the one hand, some organizational stories depict the organization as acted on by external forces to the extent that these forces either determine organizational actions or are more compatible with particular organizational forms and actions than with others. Other stories describe organizations through the actions of managers who interpret external environments and choose actions that will lead to the fulfillment of organizational goals. One story line suggests that organizations are inherently programmed, destined by history and by organizational structure to act. The other suggests that organizations are rational, intentional, and ordered, products of individual and group action (Becher and Kogan, 1992; Bennis, 1989; Crouch, Sinclair, and Hintz, 1992; Dutton and Dukerich, 1991; Hasenfeld, 1983). Not surprisingly, entire theoretical frameworks for the examination of organizations are grounded in the assumption of internal direction, and others are grounded in the assumption of external control (Dutton and Dukerich, 1991). But organizational behaviors and actions do not conveniently fit into one category or the other.

Broad appeals for organizational change are endemic in organizational literature, and this has especially been the case for the past two decades. Such appeals are based on assumptions that are questionable. These include the assumption that powerful leaders can alter existing patterns of organizational life and change how organizations act. They also include the assumption that radical or transformative change is, if not commonplace, then at least desirable. Ignored in such assumptions are not only the views that reject organizations as rational and controllable entities but also the judgment that forces promoting change outweigh those promoting stability and homeostasis (Hasenfeld, 1983; Mintzberg, 1994).

These assumptions are central to the literature on the community college over the past two decades. Advocates of the community college present the institution as the premier educational innovator of the twentieth century: they refer to the growth of these institutions and their ability to adapt through what is called "innovation" (Frye, 1994). Those critical of the institution characterize the community college as either in need of alteration to improve its performance or failing to live up to its promise because it has strayed from its traditional values (Cohen and Brawer, 1996; Dougherty, 1994; Frye, 1994; McGrath and Spear, 1991). Yet the assumption that community colleges are rational organizations that can be guided and directed by managers and designers in mechanistic fashion (Mintzberg, 1994; Morgan, 1986) ignores not only the human and unpredictable side of organizational life but also the social and political side of organizations, where meanings are constructed and negotiated. There is evidence to suggest that community colleges, more so than elite universities or four-year colleges, possess characteristics such as administrative dominance and environmental vulnerability (Baldridge, Curtis, Ecker, and Riley, 1978; Birnbaum, 1988). Nonetheless, there is little empirical evidence to indicate that community colleges are more internally directed than other organizations or that managers are strategists, acting to position their institutions favorably or adapting them to their advantage.

This examination is based on interviews with over two hundred administrators, faculty, staff, students, and board members at six community colleges in the United States and Canada during 1996 and 1997. In analyzing these interviews, I use a cultural framework that explores both the sense making of organizational members and the meanings suggested by members' articulations. That is, how do organizational members understand organizational change in their institution, and what are the explanations for these understandings?

Organizational members included college board members, the chief executive officer or president, senior administrators including vice presidents and deans, departmental chairs, full-time and part-time faculty from various instruction and service areas, support staff, and students including full-time and part-time students and student government officials.

Interviews covered topics related to institutional change, with emphasis on large, macro, external forces such as economic, political, and social forces. For example, the role of government in influencing the institution was explored, as was the role of local communities. Interviews were analyzed through identification and explication of responses that suggested either internal or external forces of change. In particular, my analysis coded interview data based on pattern coding (Miles and Huberman, 1984). I highlighted major changes identified at each institution and connected organizational members' explanations to these changes.

The Institutions

All six institutions are located in the western United States or western Canada. These institutions as a whole reflect a variety of characteristics—size, location, programming, structure—that not only might account for a number of variables of change but also might permit generalizability. For the purpose of maintaining the anonymity of each college, I have given the institutions fictitious names.

City Central College is a large institution in the heart of an urban environment. The college has a curricular emphasis on vocational training and adult basic education. In the early 1990s, the college had a third campus, but that campus separated and became an independent college.

East Shoreline College is a mid-sized college located between two major population centers. The college has one major campus and several regional campuses. In the late 1980s, the college's curricula shifted from a balanced emphasis among academic, vocational, and adult basic education to a dominant emphasis on academic education. In the 1990s, the college developed several baccalaureate degree programs.

City South Community College is a relatively small city college, part of a large urban district community college system. The college has one campus, with an emphasis on vocational training, adult basic education, and English as a second language, with aspirations to increase its academic programming.

Pacific Suburban Community College is a single-campus college, part of a larger state university and community college system. It is a mid-sized college specializing in academic programs and several high-profile two-year career programs. The college emphasizes its Pacific Rim orientation as well as its interdisciplinary programs.

Rural Valley College is a multicampus college, with two major campuses, a smaller third center located with a secondary school and a community facility, and an even smaller fourth center in a rented facility in a small town. In the 1990s, the college began to develop baccalaureate degree programs, but continued to give considerable attention to adult basic education and other access-oriented programs, such as English as a second language.

Suburban Valley Community College, with one campus, is part of a two-college district located in fairly affluent communities adjacent to large urban centers. The college has a long-standing national reputation as an innovative institution, with emphasis on academic programs, although recently there has been growth in the program areas of adult basic education and English as a second language. Nonetheless, college resources support advanced technology-oriented programs.

The Theme of External Determinism

A substantial portion of the descriptions and explanations of college members about organizational change favor the role of the external environment. At City Central College, government intervention, government funding behaviors, government policies, particularly social policy, and other government and agency actions are viewed as precipitators of organizational change. The government is accused of "micromanaging" the institution, of "buffering" the institution from the marketplace, and of affecting the institution with its practices of social equality. According to one adult basic education administrator, "Changes originate from . . . government funding patterns [and from] other government programs—that is, deinstitutionalizing mental health clients and moving them into the community, integrating disabled students into primary and secondary education classes and then the expectation is that they will move into postsecondary institutions."

East Shoreline College organizational members decry government funding policy, which does not support the kind of growth that the college is experiencing. Thus, the college has become increasingly market-oriented, pursuing resources through international contracts and through profitmaking tuition charges to foreign students. At City South Community College organizational members identify the district chief executive officer, the system chancellor, as one of the primary sources of organizational change, from restructuring of the institution to micromanaging its operations. Faculty and administrators at Pacific Suburban Community College frequently refer to the actions of the community college system chancellor and the university system president as affecting college behaviors (both community college and university are part of one higher education system). For example, their decision to move basic or remedial education programming from credit to noncredit affected the college in several ways, not least among them being higher tuition for students and a changed professional status and salary for faculty involved in the program. Both faculty and administrators at Suburban Valley Community College describe the district chancellor and the vice chancellors as powerful forces attempting to form the future path of the college. In all cases of external influencers who are district administrators or government officials, college members see these influencers as malevolent forces, acting on their institution in a negative way.

Less personal attributions are also noted as influences of the external environment. Organizational members at Pacific Suburban Community College focus on the state's economy, driven by tourism, as the critical factor of organizational action and change: a recent downturn in the tourist industry is directly connected not only to constraints on budgets but also to loss of staff positions and movement of programs from credit-based to non-credit-based so that they can become self-funded. Rural Valley College faculty and administrators cite the provincial faculty union and government relations and subsequent actions as key determiners of the destiny of the college; in particular, the two parties forged a provincewide collective bargaining agreement that places considerable stress on the college's budget. Faculty, administrators, and the chair of the board of governors at Suburban Valley Community College reiterate that the image of the college as an outstanding institution and nationally acclaimed community college has driven the college to emphasize high technology, constrain growth in the academic and basic education areas, and devote major resources to facilities and equipment that support an innovative, high-technology image.

College officials—administrators, faculty, and support staff—speak with certainty about their changing student populations. New immigrants and refugees, secondary school "dropouts," welfare participants, returning workers and laid off workers, as well as an employed workforce requiring upgrading skills, compose the community colleges, seemingly as the new majority. This population is viewed as stimulating major changes in the organization. At City South Community College, for example, the entire student services area of the college was reorganized, relocated, and refurbished to provide "one stop services." The population is also characterized as highly diverse. Growth in English as a second language programs and adult basic education are attributed to new immigrant populations located in proximity to the colleges.

Electronic technology is identified by college personnel as transforming: "The world will never be the same; connections are easier, cheaper, faster." (information technology administrator). Faculty are viewed as divided into camps: those who embrace new technologies and see opportunities for innovation, and those who are reluctant to alter what they do for fear of losing what they value. Groups of faculty and administrators at colleges connect new technologies with changing student demographics and student learning differences.

These technologies, such as computers for word processing, voice mail, electronic mail, and other communications and broadcast technologies, have not only altered delivery of instruction, most notably in self-paced programming and distance education, but also redefined worker roles. Administrators and faculty work as their own support staff, lessening the need for clerical assistance, but at the same time accommodating a much larger personal workload than in the past. There are also stories at each institution about actual or impending elimination of support staff positions. In describing a recent restructuring of City South Community College, administrators, faculty, and support staff indicated that dozens of staff positions were eliminated to save money and "streamline operations." But the net result was that administrators and other support staff took over the work formerly done by other staff.

The major recipients of new technologies are students. Personnel at every college claimed that electronic technologies were applied to student learning and services. Distance learning through the Internet and electronic mail, through two-way interactive video, and through satellite broadcast television enabled greater student access to programs. Communications technologies led to telephone and on-line registration, to on-line information about college processes, program and course requirements, and curricula. Programs in writing both at the basic level and the advanced composition level were areas most frequently cited as exploiting electronic technologies for student learning.

Numerous college employees at all colleges also indicated that expectations were considerable for their institutions to "keep up," to use new technologies, but that institutional resources and staff expertise were not keeping pace. Faculty and particularly administrators at Suburban Valley Community College stressed the point that unless their institution maintained its reputation as a leader in the use of electronic technologies, students would go elsewhere. And loss of students means loss of government revenues.

The Theme of Internal Control

A parallel explanation of organizational change is found in the view of organizational members that individuals and groups within the institution are responsible for organizational actions. In some cases, individuals and groups are seen as preservers of traditions and practices; in other cases, they are viewed as resisters to progress; and, in other cases, they are viewed as agents of change. Faculty-dominated bodies, such as senates or academic councils, are viewed as preservers of the traditions and values of the institutions by both faculty and administrators. Local faculty unions and specific faculty groupings, by department or by longevity of service, are judged by both faculty and administrators as resisters to progress. And specific administrators and faculty are viewed as agents of change.

The college president and the dean of instruction at Pacific Suburban Community College are noted, particularly by faculty, as agents of change: their biases in programming are evident to both administrators and faculty. At City South Community College, the president's approach to college decision making, which is highly participatory and consultative, is contrasted by all employee groups to the former president's approach, which was referred to as autocratic, and it is claimed to be a major change in how the college operates, underlining the importance of the formal campus leader in institutional actions. At City Central College, the governing board of the college is identified by all employee groups as a major influencer, not just in policy matters but also in what issues the college addresses and in adopting a pro-union stance. Faculty, support staff, and administrators at East Shoreline College view the faculty-dominated academic council or senate as the principal precipitator of fundamental change in how the institution is managed and in institutional processes. Before the existence of a senate, the college was seen as managed and led by a group of senior administrators, headed by the college president; since the establishment of the senate, the entire administrative group including the senior executives take direction from the senate, and the college is increasingly viewed as an institution where there is comanagement and shared governance. At Rural Valley College, the senior management group initiates change, although factions in this group help to shape the implementation of college policy and operational decisions.

College administrators see themselves and are seen by other organizational members as strategists and decision makers. Both positive and negative characterizations, such as altruistic and selfish connotations, accompany these attributions, although none are viewed as malevolent, unlike some of the external influencers.

Faculty bodies, particularly the faculty senate or the faculty-dominated council, are viewed by all employee groups as the moral center of the institution, affecting organizational change by preserving traditions and values. Only at one college, East Shoreline College, where the academic council was viewed by all groups as a dominating force, did administrators question and criticize the influence of such a body.

Local faculty unions and faculty groups are viewed by all employee groups as influential, but primarily as resisters to change initiated or proposed by administrators. Local unions endeavor to preserve jobs and increase salaries, to curtail the influence of administrators as a group or as individuals, and to gain or maintain power over organizational actions. Faculty groups, particularly those who have a long career at the college, spanning twenty to thirty years, are viewed by administrators as an opposing force intent on protecting themselves and on resisting change.

Local unions that are district or system unions have less influence over management at the institution than autonomous unions. This is the case for Pacific Suburban Community College and City South Community College, where local faculty union officials have aligned themselves with the college administration in dealing with either a system or a district's influence. At Suburban Valley Community College, where union members are part of a district union, and district union leadership is housed on the Suburban Valley campus, no specific animosity is expressed between union leadership and college administration. The union does not align itself with the college in reaction to the district, but has fewer words of disdain for college administrators than for district officers.

Explanations of Descriptions of Influence and Control

Several observations and hypotheses aid in explaining how organizational members describe influence and control in the colleges.

Managers are limited in the objective manipulation of the environment; instead they function symbolically, manipulating and managing institutional interpretations of events and meanings of organizational actions. For example, in the budgeting process, over 90 percent of college budgets are already committed, largely for employee salaries. The flexibility and influence of managers over expenditures is thus limited to small decisions. A college with a $30 million budget has often less than $3 million and more often between two and three hundred thousand dollars of discretionary funds. With multiple demands on the funds and numerous individual players and several interest groups involved, there are few actual dollars relative to the total budget that might contribute to change. Thus, managers are required to choose areas that are symbolic to support with limited funds if they are to exercise influence and be seen to control organizational actions. At Pacific Suburban Community College, the college president endeavors to commit discretionary funds to facilities improvement because the campus is regarded by the local community as well as by organizational members as a beautiful campus, and this beauty is one if its outstanding characteristics. At Suburban Valley Community College, the college administrators debate over the use of discretionary funds to provide staff support for electronic technology because there is state-of-the-art equipment but little expertise to support and service the equipment. If the college is to maintain its image as a leading institution in innovation, it cannot fall behind in its use of electronic technology.

The community college is a part of a system of community colleges, other postsecondary institutions, other social and service organizations, and government agencies, and this context—its particular system identity—is a main influence over its actions. The looser the system—that is, the more loosely coupled the system— the greater the internal control over organizational actions. Greater systems controls, whether through district central offices or through government agencies, suggest the stronger influence of the external environment on the institution. This is the case with Pacific Suburban Community College, part of a state community college and university system, where decisions from the state government and from the system central office frame and direct college actions. The clearest example of this is the decision to change adult basic education programs from credit to noncredit, a decision not made at the college level, and apparently not influenced by internal constituents.

The more the college personnel assume that there is a system and system controls, the less they will perceive their institution as having control over its own actions or the ability to commit the institution to specific actions. The importance of perception and the definition of institutional identity follows from the view of systems influence described above. This is clearly the case with City Central College, where organizational members see an oppressive system in the form of an intrusive government, and where there are few areas of choice for the college in committing itself to actions. It has narrowed its mission not only to serve its local population but also to ensure that it has the ability to control this mission and its attendant goals.

Environmental changes either stimulate colleges to respond or are ignored by colleges through rationalizations. Colleges that respond choose strategies that fit their identity framework—how they are perceived and perceive themselves as institutions. These strategies thus serve to reinforce that identity if they are perceived as successful and contradict and even change that identity if they are perceived as unsuccessful. College decision makers ignore environmental changes when they do not perceive themselves as capable of responding or because they see these changes as inconsistent with their present identity or the identity they may acquire by responding. Although administrators at Suburban Valley Community College sense that their student population is altering and that there is growing demand for academic programs and English as a second language programs, they try to ignore or diminish the significance of these environmental alterations. Instead, the college administrators attend to the image of the college as an innovative, high-technology institution and work at boosting college enrollments in technology-related fields.

Internal influences over organizational change are contained in existing structures that combine these influences with institutional history, culture, and symbols as well as the organization's stage of development. This influence is not a conscious, rational choice of individual actors, but it may play out as an internal response to external forces that generate internal change. Constrained government funding and increasing demand for services lead Rural Valley College's administrators not to cut services but to increase them by locating alternative sources of revenues. Rural Valley has a tradition of positive employee relations, few union grievances, and almost no layoffs. To cut services to match government revenues would mean reduction of the workforce, an action counter to the college's pattern of behavior. Thus, the college managers alter college operational philosophy to a more enterprising approach so that Rural Valley can maintain its mission of serving students. The college managers and faculty pursue international students to gain a profit, and college activity expands in the contract services area to garner additional revenues.

Conclusions

From these stories and explanations, it is clear that both the external and internal environments have roles in organizational change. Organizations are neither solely influenced and altered by external forces nor directed and controlled by internal managers or other internal individuals or groups. The actions of organizations are neither totally determined by external forces nor fully influenced by internal forces. These stories and explanations as a whole suggest that organizational change is the interplay between external and internal forces, between the perceptions of internal members of organizational identity and the external environment and between the organizational fit with the external environment and organizational symbols that match environmental needs. Community colleges are not static organizations: they alter, change their approaches, their programs, and their relationship with their environment. But they are not transformed institutions; they have not become another institution: they are neither universities nor secondary schools; they are neither corporations nor small businesses. They possess the attributes of many other organizations; they do so because on the one hand their external environment pushes them in that direction, and on the other hand because in order to survive yet maintain their purposes, community colleges themselves change course and adopt new approaches, new technologies, and new employees.

The descriptions and explanations of organizational members about their institution reflect the subjective and often shared meanings of organizational members that enable them to understand daily events and assist them with action (Morgan, 1986). These descriptions and explanations are like stories told after the event or experience in an attempt to fit it in a framework of understanding that gives sense to action. Explanations of organizational change in the community college, then, are sense-making devices for members to shape the identity of their institutions.

References

Astley, W. "Administrative Science as Socially Constructed Truth." *Administrative Science Quarterly,* 1985, *30,* 497–513.

Baldridge, V., Curtis, D., Ecker, G., and Riley, G. *Policy Making and Effective Leadership.* San Francisco: Jossey-Bass, 1978.

Becher, T., and Kogan, M. *Process and Structure in Higher Education.* New York: Routledge, 1992.

Bennis, W. *Why Leaders Can't Lead: The Unconscious Conspiracy Continues.* San Francisco: Jossey-Bass, 1989.

Birnbaum, R. *How Colleges Work: The Cybernetics of Academic Organization and Leadership.* San Francisco: Jossey-Bass, 1991.

Cohen, A. M., and Brawer, F. B. *The American Community College* (3rd ed.) San Francisco: Jossey-Bass, 1996.

Crouch, A., Sinclair, A., and Hintz, P. "Myths of Managing Change." In D. Hosking and N. Anderson (eds.), *Organizational Change and Innovation: Psychological Perspectives and Practices in Europe.* New York: Routledge, 1992.

Dougherty, K. *The Contradictory College*. Albany: State University of New York Press, 1994.

Dutton, J., and Dukerich, J. "Keeping an Eye on the Mirror: Image and Identity in Organizational Adaptation." *Academy of Management Journal,* 1991, *34* (3), 517–554.

Frye, J. "Educational Paradigms in the Professional Literature of the Community College." In J. Smart (ed.), *Higher Education: Handbook of Theory and Research,* vol. 10. New York: Agathon Press, 1994.

Hasenfeld, Y. *Human Service Organizations*. Englewood Cliffs, N.J.: Prentice Hall, 1983.

McGrath, D., and Spear, M. *The Academic Crisis of the Community College*. Albany: State University of New York Press, 1991.

Miles, M., and Huberman, M. *Qualitative Data Analysis: A Sourcebook of New Methods*. Beverly Hills, Calif.: Sage Publications, 1984.

Mintzberg, H. *The Rise and Fall of Strategic Planning*. New York: Free Press, 1994.

Morgan, G. *Images of Organization*. Beverly Hills, Calif.: Sage Publications, 1986.

Pfeffer, J. *Organizations and Organization Theory*. Marshfield, Mass.: Pitman, 1982.

JOHN STEWART LEVIN is director of the Community College Institute and associate professor of higher education at the Center for the Study of Higher Education, The University of Arizona.

Critics of higher education such as Michael Dolence and Donald Norris (1995) urge educators to transform their institutions so as to align them with the needs of the twenty-first-century learner. However, colleges desiring to survive and thrive in a rapidly changing external environment often discover they must first find a way to make fundamental changes in their institutional culture.

Managing Change: A Case Study in Evolving Strategic Management

Linda Thor, Carol Scarafiotti, Laura Helminski

Organizational culture has been defined by Schein (in Bergquist, 1992) as a "pattern of basic assumptions that a given group has invented, discovered or developed in learning to cope with its problems of external adaptation and internal integration, and that has worked well enough to be considered valid, and therefore, to be taught to new members as the correct way to perceive, think, and feel in relation to those problems" (p. 2). Another definition characterizes culture in higher education as "collective, mutually shaping patterns of norms, values, practices, beliefs and assumptions that guide the behavior of individuals and groups and provide a frame of reference within which to interpret the meaning of events and actions on and off campus" (Kuh, Schuh, and Whitt, 1991, p. 19). A common thread, then, is that an organization's culture includes unique attitudes, values, and practices learned by its members. The authors of this chapter assert that organizations desiring to foster cultures that are both current and aligned with the requirements of a rapidly changing world should adopt an evolving and strategic management model.

To illustrate the concept of evolving strategic management, this chapter presents a case study. It examines how and why Rio Salado College (Rio) in Tempe, Arizona, radically changed its culture and its form as it adopted the Total Quality Management (TQM) philosophy, and how and why it later modified its TQM management model to establish, instead, an evolving strategic management approach based on Senge's (1990) learning organization. Equally important, this chapter also explains the implications of making changes in an institution's culture, processes, and form, illustrating how a change in one area precipitated other changes.

Rio's first experience, a formal, planned, collegewide movement to implement TQM, ultimately resulted in major changes in the college's culture, practices, mission, and vision. Its subsequent experience, a continuous movement to become a learning organization, involved a subtler, more informal management approach designed to inculcate evolution in the thinking and interactions of all employees rather than to change the college's mission or form. The two experiences together have enabled the college to survive grave internal and external threats, and to find a stance by which it can respond successfully to a future that is arriving at breakneck speed. Although Rio can be classified as a "distinctive college" (Townsend and others, 1992, p. 1) because of its unique nature, its experiences can provide helpful insights to other colleges contemplating how to deal with a rapidly changing environment.

The Original Organization

Rio Salado College was established in 1978 as a unique community college. It was designed specifically to serve Maricopa County's underserved geographical areas and populations through nontraditional means. In other words, its mandate was to meet community needs unmet by the then six community colleges composing the county's community college district. Rio would not have a campus but instead would lease facilities in strategic areas of the county. Also, Rio would employ mainly administrators and adjunct faculty.

From its inception, the college was designed to be an agent of change, an innovator in the use of instructional technology, and a producer of low-cost ·enrollments. Reflecting its decentralized structure—eight regional offices created to provide instructional and support services to target geographical areas—the college adopted a decentralized, internally competitive, strategic management approach designed to encourage and reward independent action. The approach worked well for twelve years. Each regional office was perceived by its chief administrators and staff as an autonomous minicampus. Each sought to provide comprehensive services and programs to its target population. Each thrived as an independent entrepreneurial unit whose bottom-line goal was to increase enrollment, and growth was rewarded by budget increases.

Throughout these early years, Rio employees demonstrated a pioneering spirit as well as an internally competitive drive, both of which spawned innovation and growth. For example, the college broke away from the traditional sixteen-week semester. Instead, the individual regional offices offered courses and programs on schedules that were convenient for the communities they served. Regional offices also developed a variety of "fast track," accelerated programs customized for special populations such as residents of the nearby U.S. Air Force base. Moreover, the college was the first Maricopa County community college to offer registration by telephone. The Distance Learning program, started in 1978, also took hold. No doubt as a result of these innovations, the college's enrollment grew.

As the college matured, however, its decentralized form and internally competitive culture became increasingly less effective and more problematic. First, although the college had espoused an official mission, the missions of the eight autonomous regional offices soon superseded it in practice. In other words, operationally the college lacked a common, or shared, mission and vision. Second, students were confused by eight autonomous schedules for what was supposedly one college. Third, as state funding for community colleges dwindled, the cost/benefit ratio resulting from decentralization and autonomy became increasingly less tolerable. It was difficult to utilize economy of scale in purchasing because there were few collegewide work processes and procedures. In addition, there were no collegewide training programs to develop collegewide employee capacity; instead, there were eight local programs. Fourth, inadvertently, Rio had perpetuated the perception of itself as a college of second choice. With its decentralization, it could not attract enough students to warrant offering comprehensive education programs; therefore, it focused on providing courses rather than programs. Students attracted to Rio were drawn mainly because they needed a single course in a convenient location.

In addition to problems created by the internally competitive management model, two major changes in the external environment threatened the college's survival. Within twelve years, the number of Maricopa County community colleges had increased from six to ten, each providing services to geographical areas served by Rio. Thus, Rio, the community college that had once thrived by meeting the needs of underserved geographical areas, now saw its market shrink significantly. In addition, over the years, Rio's competitor community colleges had begun to adopt many of the innovations that once had been unique to Rio. As a result, Rio faced fierce competition both externally and internally. Rio Salado College administrators and faculty soon realized that for the college to survive over the long term, it had to make some changes.

The Adoption of Total Quality Management

In 1990, the newly appointed president of Rio Salado College, Linda Thor, encouraged the college leadership to explore the potential of TQM as a vehicle to drive needed internal reform. She believed that much as it had helped corporate institutions, a TQM culture could help educational institutions survive in the coming new century.

Although TQM dates from its use in the 1950s in Japan, this philosophy took hold relatively recently in the United States, in the 1980s and 1990s, when corporations struggled for new ways to survive in a harshly competitive society composed of demanding consumers. Briefly, the TQM philosophy and principles focus all the organization's behaviors and resources on the goal of meeting and exceeding the customer's expectations. Along with its strong customer orientation, several other characteristics highlight TQM: reducing variation and error in processes, viewing each employee as an internal customer, empowering employees and teams, emphasizing continuous, incremental improvement, encouraging prevention rather than inspection, and using tools and data for problem solving and decision making (Deming, 1982).

The idea of TQM as a strategic management model was for the most part well received at Rio. In early 1991, the president hired an outside consultant to provide extensive TQM training to an initial leadership group comprising selected administrators, faculty, and staff, and to help the college design an implementation strategy. Critical to the successful implementation of TQM was the commitment and involvement throughout the adoption phase by executive management, faculty, and staff leaders. As Merron (1994) notes, the top level of an organization must lead in the commitment and alignment to TQM in order to achieve optimal performance. Middle managers had the greatest misgivings about TQM. In the old competitive structure they held the power in their small decentralized fiefdoms, and they competed against each other for growth and resource allocation. In essence, they believed that they had the most to lose by a change in culture and structure. However, although the TQM philosophy was antithetical to their culture of rivalry, middle managers also realized that the college needed to make some changes. Thus, they supported the implementation of TQM.

Implementation also included adopting a collegewide TQM strategic management model consisting of several formal parts. Overseeing the institution was a TQM Strategic Planning and Steering Team established to ensure that the anticipated internal changes would further the college's vision and mission. Next, official Continuous Improvement Teams (CITs) were created under the auspices of the TQM Steering Team. These involved employees from throughout the organization who were trained to serve as members of teams and who came together to work on process improvement. Within each CIT, members were assigned specific roles such as "coach" and "process owner," and each CIT followed a prescribed improvement cycle. Finally, a Quality Coordinator served as liaison between the TQM Steering Team and the CITs.

Equally important to successful TQM implementation was a major, formal, collegewide training component. At an early stage, the college decided that it would be necessary to move as quickly as possible from external trainers, or the consultants who were hired in 1991, to internal trainers. Internal trainers reduced costs, but more importantly they helped to infuse the new philosophy into the institutional culture. For that reason, these training teams, each with five to seven individuals, were drawn from the ranks of working administrators, faculty, and staff, not from an existing training department. Their job, essentially, was to adapt the corporate TQM philosophy and principles to meet the academy's needs.

Significantly, when the leadership of Rio Salado College adopted the TQM philosophy, they also realized that to make the TQM approach work to its fullest capacity, the college's operating structure would have to change. They saw that the old, internally competitive, decentralized structure could not be a sound foundation for a management philosophy based on cooperation among internal customers, teamwork, and a shared vision. The old organization was fragmented to the extent that it was difficult even to identify major cross-organizational critical processes, let alone collaborate to achieve common goals.

In effect, then, implementing TQM actually led to a major reorganization. Members of the TQM Steering Team transformed the college to coordinate its philosophy and its practice. The old, independent regional offices headed by middle managers were replaced by units that provided major collegewide programs, functions, and services, all of which were interdependent. The new structure promoted internal cooperation and discouraged internal competition. The focus of the institution began to shift to meeting the needs of customers and staying ahead of external competitors.

As more employees were schooled in TQM, a new culture began to emerge, with work ethics and practices that would eventually enable Rio Salado not only to survive but also to thrive. This culture had several major characteristics. The first was a new emphasis on work teams. Previously, each department or area considered itself a nearly autonomous working body; rarely did members of one department interact with members of another. However, the TQM philosophy encouraged the formation of cross-functional, vertically integrated teams to improve processes and to solve problems. The cross-functional team concept had a profound effect on Rio's culture and continues to be the preferred method for working on collegewide challenges.

A second characteristic of the new culture was a change in college values. As a result of TQM, the college came to place a strong emphasis on service, quality, and continuous improvement rather than on merely increasing student enrollment. Involved in discussions that ranged beyond accomplishing their specific work tasks, employees now began to focus on continually improving the quality of their work. This new orientation fundamentally changed how work was perceived in order to accomplish the college's vision and mission. The consequence was that people were enthusiastic in their efforts to improve and no longer focused on only the bottom line. Moreover, discussions about values continued across departmental and area lines.

The third significant characteristic of the new culture was a shared understanding of the meaning of customer service. Most employees came to understand the importance of thinking first of the customer's needs and expectations, not about how much work was or was not getting done. Employees came to place high value on serving the customer well, and their new attitude often served as a catalyst for making procedural changes. As employees began to see students as external customers and each other as internal customers, they came to be willing to examine the needs of both groups and to change outmoded or dysfunctional processes. Examples of successful employee-developed improvements included streamlining the college and district purchasing process, making the catalogue common pages more user friendly, and designing and revising a collegewide rewards and recognition process.

A final critical step in the college's structural transformation was the revision of its mission. Previously, the job of drafting a mission statement was assumed to be the responsibility of the top leadership. Now it was seen as a task that allowed all employees to contribute to drafting the college's mission. The new mission statement focuses on Rio's unique and customized programs, accelerated programs, and courses and programs for delivery by distance technologies.

It took four years for the TQM philosophy, principles, and tools to become part of the college's culture. In that period, TQM was embraced by employees and provided the framework for the way in which the college conducted business. Employees knew what to do when they wanted to make a change or solve a problem: they applied a tool or used the process improvement cycle: "plan, do, check, act." Because everyone had been trained in the use of the TQM tools, there now existed a common vocabulary.

The Case for Continuing Change

An institution's culture is dynamic. As Morgan notes, "Culture is constantly evolving, incorporating changes in the values, beliefs, and attitudes of the external environment as well as those of institutional members" (in Kuh, Schuh, and Whitt, 1991, p. 71). Predictably, then, some of the conditions that caused the college to embrace the TQM philosophy and management model were themselves changed, and new needs arose. Destructive internal competition had indeed declined. And formidable external competition had increased.

In particular, the college needed better, faster innovation. It needed everyone to respond to major advances in technology so that the college could compete with a variety of local, national, and international public and private colleges and teaching organizations, all interested in obtaining a share of the distance learner market. New organizations such as Western Governors University, the International Community College, and Arizona Learning Systems posed a threat to a college that once had the local distance learning market to itself.

However, when innovation was most needed, it did not happen, because too many of the college's resources were allocated to Rio's self-imposed version of TQM formalities rather than to the production of important outcomes. For example, the TQM Steering Team and its official CITs that had worked well initially had become a lumbering, bureaucratic system that could neither produce results fast enough nor answer the need for large-scale innovation. TQM Steering Team meetings became mired in process trivia, and members of the TQM Steering Team who viewed their time as not well utilized stopped attending the meetings.

Eventually, the Steering Team dissolved. Although the concept of the process improvement cycle was adopted throughout the college and continues in use today, official Continuous Improvement Teams were too often caught up in the ritual surrounding the use of the process improvement cycle. In retrospect, the outcome rarely justified the time and resource commitment required to produce it. In short, official CITs frequently lost sight of their goals because they perceived using the tools and attending meetings to be their main focus. It is interesting to note that Rio's problem with the bureaucracy of TQM teams is relatively common. For example, Brigham (1993) indicates that often teams become bogged down when there is confusion about objectives and about deadlines for completion.

The demise of the TQM management model, therefore, taught the college a valuable lesson and, together with momentous external developments, presented a new challenge. Instead of adopting another management model with a formal structure, the college leadership learned that it needed a strategic management approach capable of evolving with a dynamic culture and able to position the college to deal adeptly with rapid external change.

Becoming a Learning Organization

Thus, in 1994, the Rio Salado College leadership asked two questions: What step will help the college maintain a competitive edge? What management model will enable the college to take that step? They found answers in Senge's concept of the learning organization: "A Learning Organization is a place where people continually expand their capacity to create its future, where adaptive learning is joined by generative learning" (Senge, 1990, p. 14).

Senge's "Five Disciplines of a Learning Organization" (Exhibit 6.1) also seemed to be a good fit with the college's needs and with its TQM foundation. Moreover, the concept seemed to point the way to take the organization to the next level.

Exhibit 6.1. Peter Senge's Five Disciplines of a Learning Organization

Personal mastery. Learning to expand our personal capacity to create desired results, and creating a culture that encourages all members to develop so that they can achieve their goals and purposes.

Mental models. Continually reflecting on, clarifying, and improving our internal pictures of the world and noticing how they shape our actions and decisions.

Shared visions. Building group commitment by developing shared images of the future we seek to create and the principles and guiding practices by which we expect to get there.

Team learning. Transforming conversational and collective thinking skills so that groups can reliably develop intelligence and ability greater than the sum of their individual members' talents.

Systems thinking. Learning a new way of thinking about, describing, and understanding the forces and interrelationships that shape the behavior of systems, to see how to change systems effectively, and to act in tune with the larger natural and economic processes.

Source: Senge and others, 1994, p. 6.

It is important here to emphasize the difference between change and evolution. When the college embraced the TQM philosophy, it altered itself radically. When it adopted the learning organization approach, however, the college began a gradual evolution that builds on its TQM foundation rather than departing sharply from it. That is, those who are committed to the college's becoming a learning organization would not have supported the move in that direction if they had not already experienced the changes brought about by the shift to the TQM model. TQM emphasized shared mission and vision, customer service, teamwork, understanding process, empowering employees, continuous improvement, and strategically aligned resources. The resulting conceptual infrastructure enabled the leadership to envision a culture in which all employees would increase their capacity to create and innovate continually, and in which they could design new systems without allowing old structures to limit their thinking.

This evolving strategic management model is characterized by inculcating the five disciplines and by accepting dynamism rather than imposing rigid, formal management systems. The new model allows the institutional culture to reinforce valued fundamentals as it discards outmoded ways and adopts new processes. What is important is the learning that comes from the growth and movement that the model encourages. The model is not limited by structure; it is expanded and enhanced by the behaviors embodied in the five disciplines of the learning organization.

The college's evolution toward becoming a learning organization began with a change that reflects the new values. When the TQM Steering Team was discontinued, a new meeting format quickly took its place: the Leadership Council. Members of the TQM Steering Team who had become discouraged by the tediousness of the Steering Team agendas took the lead to form a leadership community with a different goal: to share research, to engage in dialogue, and to learn. Leadership Council meetings are currently opportunities to teach each other about new theories and concepts, such as Wheatley's (1994) chaos theory and Howe and Strauss's (1993) "thirteenth generation." Through this mechanism, college leadership pursues the role of learner, indicating, as one member put it, that this role feels "right for the organization." The fifteen members of the TQM Steering Team represented all employee groups of the college—administration, faculty, and staff. The newly formed Leadership Council had twenty-five members from the same three employee groups.

Given the emphases in the institution on Senge's model, it is significant that the evolution toward becoming a learning organization has been different from the earlier shift to the TQM model. The implementation of the TQM philosophy was expansive and involved all employees in formal training and practice. Evolving into a learning organization has involved less formal planning and a more spontaneous "just in time" approach. Several faculty and administrators who were interested in learning organization concepts have become resident experts on ideas from Peter Senge's books *The Fifth Discipline* (1990) and

The Fifth Discipline Fieldbook (Senge and others, 1994). They lead discussions on various readings, videos, and satellite conferences, all associated with learning organization concepts. They also provide practice sessions for those who want to learn Senge's five disciplines.

The college has recognized that the different approaches to implementation have, in fact, been key to their success. As noted, TQM implementation was formal, deliberately expansive, and mandatory for everyone. Implementation of the learning organization philosophy is informal, fluid (reaching employees as interest grows), and voluntary.

Yet, each philosophy has become pervasive as it meets the needs of the college as a whole. Employees respond in a different way to the learning organization culture than they did to TQM, but their acceptance is no less authentic. Their use of the learning organization vocabulary and their attempts to demonstrate skills and concepts all attest to their interest in and understanding of the learning organization. In addition to introducing key concepts, college learning organization experts assist groups in the college that are interested in applying Senge's concepts to their projects. For example, faculty who are interested in moving forward with a technology agenda spent a semester in dialogue about the learning organization. Later, a group of college middle managers having operational responsibilities for supporting college initiatives received training about learning organizations.

The cultural transformation that evolved as a result of adapting the learning organization philosophy comes from viewing the five disciplines as strategies for change. Indeed, these disciplines have taken on specific meanings at Rio Salado College. Personal mastery means the commitment to learning on the part of each employee. Perhaps the most difficult of the disciplines but perceived as the most useful in the pursuit of knowledge is mental models. As employees practice effective communication through the discipline of mental models, they have to work on examining their assumptions and beliefs to find ways to abandon outdated structures and create new ones. Shared visions means that all employees have a common perception of the college goals and understand their roles in achieving the college's purposes. Team learning has brought about a major improvement in the effectiveness of college teams; it means that merely working well as a team is not enough: now the goal is to learn together so that teams can create and innovate. Systems thinking has also had a major effect. It means that college personnel must be aware that they cannot simply think within their segregated functions. Rather, they must recognize the implications of their work for the larger system. Systems thinking has been especially important as teams work on innovations.

The learning organization philosophy offers the college deeper and richer dialogue than did TQM, which was more concrete and process oriented. There were times when the college leadership thought that TQM conversations became too focused on detail. Also, those who are involved in practicing the disciplines of a learning organization find themselves responding with enthusiasm at being learners, which is not the usual role for administrators and

faculty. And the learning organization philosophy enables the college to create, design, and innovate more effectively as team members become proficient
in examining mental models and in team learning. Nonetheless, the learning
organization approach is driven by the top of the organization. That is, the
work of transformation is carried on primarily by administrators and faculty
at this point. By contrast, even early in TQM, all employees were active.

Early Outcomes

The premise of equifinality is that there are always multiple causes for any
effect. Therefore, it is impossible to prove empirically that Rio Salado College's
current enrollment success (see Table 6.1) is the direct result of its evolved
TQM and learning organization management strategy. However, it is evident
that because of the college's strong emphasis on customer service, Rio has been
able to cultivate new student markets by establishing partnerships with business and government. Also, the college has been able to move more quickly
than competitor colleges to respond to such opportunities, in part because of
its strong dedication to shared vision and its work with mental models. These
skills and values have helped the college to transcend the traditional communication barriers between faculty and administration, and as a result the ener-
gies of the college can be focused on innovation, customer service, and
providing students with positive learning experiences.

Similarly, because of its focus on systems thinking, the college has been
able to innovate quickly and to elicit support for innovations from across the
college. For example, a recent major college effort involved developing courses
to be delivered through the Internet. In only one year the college developed
over seventy courses for on-line delivery and also added all the traditional college services, such as admissions, advisement, and book sales, on-line. Even
more noteworthy is the collegewide effort, begun in May 1997, in which the
college offers students the opportunity to begin any of its 142 distance-deliv-
ery courses every two weeks through the year.

Table 6.1. Growth in Full-Time Student Equivalency (FTSE)

Year	FTSE
1986–87	3,051
1987–88	3,096
1988–89	3,304
1989–90	3,650
1990–91	4,088
1991–92	3,751
1992–93	3,439
1993–94	4,078
1994–95	4,289
1995–96	4,808
1996–97	5,649

Conclusions

What can be learned from the college's experience? Although Rio Salado College is a distinctive college, its experiences are relevant to colleges desiring to manage change. The following are some lessons learned:

To meet the needs of a rapidly changing external environment, an organization should foster change in its culture.

Organizations can create desired internal change by implementing an evolving strategic management model.

An internal cultural change can create the need for additional changes in the structure and work processes of an organization.

One static management model cannot provide all that is needed to manage the numerous changes that are currently under way in the external environment. On the other hand, valued practices, theories, and beliefs will endure even if an outmoded model dissolves.

Enduring and valued practices, theories, and beliefs can be integrated into a new strategic management model.

References

Bergquist, W. H. *The Four Cultures of the Academy: Insights and Strategies for Improving Leadership in Collegiate Organizations.* San Francisco: Jossey-Bass, 1992.

Brigham, S. "TQM Lessons We Can Learn from Industry." *Change,* 1993, 25, 42–46, 48.

Deming, W. *Quality, Productivity, and Competitive Position.* Cambridge, Mass.: MIT Center for Advanced Engineering Study, 1982.

Dolence, M., and Norris, D. *Transforming Higher Education: A Vision for Learning in the Twenty-First Century.* Ann Arbor, Mich.: Society for College and University Planning, 1995.

Howe, N., and Strauss, B. *13th GEN.* New York: Vintage Books, 1993.

Kuh, G. D., Schuh, J. H., and Whitt, E. J. *Involving Colleges: Successful Approaches to Fostering Student Learning and Development Outside the Classroom.* San Francisco: Jossey-Bass, 1991.

Merron, K. "Creating TQM Organizations." *Quality Progress,* 1994, 27 (52) 51–54.

Senge, P., Kleiner, A., Roberts, C., Ross, R., and Smith, B. *The Fifth Discipline Fieldbook.* New York: Doubleday, 1994.

Senge, P. M. *The Fifth Discipline: The Art and Practice of the Learning Organization.* New York: Currency Doubleday, 1990.

Townsend, B., and others. "Creating Distinctiveness: Lessons from Uncommon Colleges and Universities." *ERIC Digest.* Washington, D.C.: ERIC Clearinghouse on Higher Education, 1992. (ED 356 753)

Wheatley, M. J. *Leadership and the New Science: Learning About Organization from an Orderly Universe.* San Francisco: Berrett-Koehler Publishers, 1994.

LINDA THOR is president, Rio Salado College, Arizona.

CAROL SCARAFIOTTI is dean of instruction, Rio Salado College, Arizona.

LAURA HELMINSKI is a faculty member of Rio Salado College, Arizona.

The current theories of Margaret Wheatley and others inform administrative behaviors that affect organizational change in a diverse urban environment.

The Urban Community College in the Midst of Change

J. Marie Pepicello, Marsha Hopkins

In this last decade of the twentieth century, urban community colleges across the country are experiencing a time of very rapid change and unique challenges. Some communities in which the population demographics are changing quickly also are home to public school systems that struggle with high dropout and low graduation rates. The charge to the urban community college, as an integral component of a complex urban system, is to define community "not only as a region to be served, but also as a climate to be created" (Boyer, 1988, p. 3).

Competing Forces

Peggy Gordon Elliott, in *The Urban Campus*, identifies two major forces or frameworks in which current urban America is developing. The first is one of technology and economics, in which advanced thinking and communication skills are required: "To compete in such an environment today, men and women must be educated, focused, highly skilled, and the best at what they do. . . . The promise of this paradigm is the real potential for people to do well, providing they are highly competent and adequately prepared for the large number of well-paying jobs that the information economy is producing" (Elliott, 1994, p. 10).

The second force discussed by Elliott is related to the rapidly changing demography of this country's urban areas, which could be characterized as bimodal. At the same time that there is a significant increase in the aging population, there is a boom in young minority populations fueled both by birthrates higher than that of Caucasians and by immigration into the urban centers. One important aspect of this demography is the concentration of poverty, unemployment, and underemployment in the urban core. "As America continues to change, the disparity between the paradigm of the competitive, technology-driven society and the paradigm of people becomes more obvious. The match is not a good one" (Elliott, 1994, p. 15).

Phoenix College, one of the Maricopa Community Colleges, is located in central Phoenix "in the heart of the city." Founded in 1920 as an alternative to lower-division university education—the University of Arizona was located a distant ninety miles away—Phoenix College has grown from its original twenty junior college students to a comprehensive community college serving about eleven thousand credit students and an additional two thousand to three thousand noncredit students per semester. The college "community" includes the state financial center; tourism and recreation sites including theaters, restaurants, and professional sports venues; the state, city, and county government centers; and residential neighborhoods, which range from some of the more exclusive in the city to some of the poorest and most troubled. In brief, this is a typical urban environment served by that uniquely American institution—a community college.

An article in the local newspaper, *The Arizona Republic,* "Central Phoenix shows signs of decline," details some of the challenges facing the area immediately surrounding Phoenix College (Padgett, 1994, p. B3). Of the city's eight council districts, District 4, in which Phoenix College is located, had the highest percentage of adults over sixty-five, high school dropouts, adults reporting abuse of a drug in the past year, and adults who have been a victim of domestic abuse. From 1980 to 1990, the population in District 4 actually decreased by 3 percent, while all other seven council districts increased in population.

Phoenix Union High School District (PUHSD), with a student population of about eighteen thousand students and eleven high schools, is the principal feeder district to Phoenix College and several of the other Maricopa colleges. About 50 percent of PUHSD graduates who enter college the fall after their high school graduation go to Phoenix College.

The school district has extraordinary challenges. On statewide standardized achievement scores in 1996, PUHSD high schools were eight of the nine lowest-ranking high schools in Arizona. In the 1995–96 academic year, 55 percent of students were Hispanic, 28 percent of students were Caucasian, and 12 percent were African American, with smaller percentages of Native American and Asian American students. The challenges, opportunities, and threats in Phoenix College's present and future are dramatic illustrations of the contrasting forces of a competitive, technology-driven society and illustrations of "the people" striving to cope with the vicissitudes of daily life.

The Search for Direction

The rapidly changing forces of our time, particularly technological changes, have brought about an ever expanding knowledge base. Keeping up with the changes does not seem possible. Trying to manage by finding a means to control change is not prudent. And ignoring change is deadly. The challenges encountered by Phoenix College in meeting changing constraints and customer needs mirror those faced by society as a whole. What should be the response is the pressing question.

Staying the Same. The search for the well-ordered organization in traditional, mechanistic settings was based on equating order with the feeling of being in control. This control came primarily from constricting and restricting information flow in the formal organization, between members informally, and between the organization and those outside it. This created a power structure where those with the information dominate.

Those members of such organizations who fear being out of control perceive strict rules, strict mandates, restriction of the flow of information on a need-to-know basis flowing top-down hierarchically, and rigid chains of command as keeping everything in control and effectively moving toward the desired end. Actually the entire organization may be operating in fear, which stifles and blocks action. If roles are not adhered to, if strict rules are not enforced, if information is not controlled, then the pyramidal structure would collapse and no one would know what to do or how to do it or would even have an identity beyond their role. The result would be chaos. As Wheatley has put it: "In organizations we typically struggle against the environment, seeing it as the source of disruption and change. We tend to insulate ourselves from it as long as possible in an effort to preserve the previous stability we have acquired" (1992, p. 90). In educational institutions, as in other organizations, the status quo gives a feeling of stability, but it is only an illusion. The system becomes fixed, locked in its rules with a restricted flow of information. Adaptation to the ever changing demographic and technological forces in this environment is limited even though efforts may be directed at trying to serve the community through education. There is change, but change in such organizations is incremental.

The New Reflection. Ralph D. Stacey, in *Complexity and Creativity in Organizations,* notes that structures, plans, cognitive perceptions, and response to experiences change first at the individual level. The individual forms the new idea and shares it. Even small changes become iterated and amplified across several others. (Stacey, 1996, p. 177). Complexity theory as presented by Waldrop (1992) and Zohar (1994) underscores this by adding that even small perturbations to the "field of possibilities" begin a ripple and are iterated and amplified. Therefore, it does not take large numbers or widespread efforts to begin to effect change.

The decision-making process in an interactive organization involves the examination of the present situation related to what went before, what may come after, and all of the players who may be affected. Decisions are also bounded by broad principles. Choices are an outgrowth of an agreed process of interacting, bounded by the broad guiding principles, and rich with information about the situation. The outcomes are not at the end of a step-by-step process but are an outgrowth of continual deliberations. The assumption is that the more alternatives there are, the more participation there will be, and the more diverse the information is, the richer and more appropriate the outcome will be.

Decisions and actions are then more responsive to today's students and to today's rapidly changing world. The organization is not seeking the right solution but one that is a close match for the situation as it is known. An important aspect of the new science is that there are an infinite number of possibilities rather than a single correct solution.

The stability of the well-ordered, adaptive organization is in its ability to identify processes by which to interact, to become aware of certain broad principles to guide all actions and decisions, and to embrace the concept that the organization operates inside out and outside in, not top down or bottom up. Flowing with and adapting to change, rather than being reactive and overreactive, are the desired behaviors.

The Interactive Organization

What is the organization that evolves from this perspective? Are there key characteristics that one could identify to know that it is operating according to newer models rather than mechanistic ones? Wheatley observes that in nature complex levels of information and resultant outcomes come from simple information being looped and fed back on itself. Furthermore, through free-flowing information the organization creates complex and new forms. The resultant structures or creative solutions are generated by simple information in interaction (Wheatley, 1992). The outcomes can be complex, but the information is not and the processes are not.

Senge, in *The Fifth Discipline,* believes that the organization is a "by-product of individual visions, a by-product of on-going conversations" (1990, p. 56). This does not necessarily mean that a group sits down and writes a vision statement, but that it is an outgrowth of continued dialogue.

We believe that the fertile environment for the ongoing, continuous change that is present in an adapting organization, one that embraces change and understands ambiguity, has these characteristics: the organization (1) is based on cooperation and values; (2) encourages interaction and is engaged in dialogue; (3) sees diversity as an asset; (4) is open with information and accepting of information and ideas; (5) is thinking and questioning continually; (6) embraces the individual and at the same time sees the individual as part of a whole; and (7) is a risk taking environment, involving new ideas, interaction with others, and self-reflection. Also, the organization (8) sees itself as operating not top down or bottom up, but as individuals with valuable points of view. Overall, the organization (9) is oriented to process and solutions, and (10) is connected to both its internal and external communities.

Phoenix College

The rich diversity of student ethnicity at Phoenix College gives some indication of the effects of the changes in the urban area (Figure 7.1). The local economy, after a recession in the late 1980s and early 1990s, entered and still continues in a very strong, robust period with steady job growth and low unemployment. The student enrollment at Phoenix College, as measured in full-time student equivalents (FTSEs), reflects a common inverse relationship with the economy by growth in the early 1990s and then decline (Figure 7.2).

Figure 7.1. Phoenix College Enrollment History

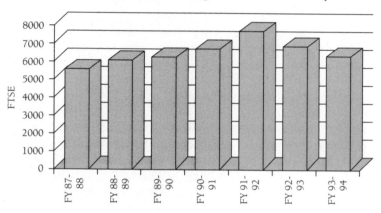

Figure 7.2. Phoenix College Student Ethnicity, 1996

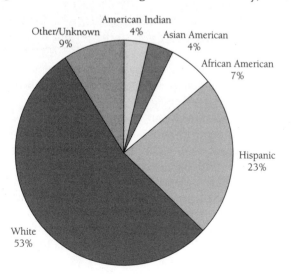

When a new president, one of the authors, arrived at Phoenix College in the summer of 1993, her assessment of the college was that there were great strengths, including a student-centered culture, a high standard for classroom teaching, a long history, many alumni who are proud of their association with the college, and a physical plant that is attractive and distinctive in its traditional architecture. The assessment also revealed formidable challenges: enrollment had dropped significantly since 1991–92; the buildings, equipment, and plant infrastructure were in serious need of a major infusion of capital funding; there was little activity in program development; and the campus climate was described by a college planning consultant in 1990 as "a risk-averse atmosphere which reduces creativity and innovation throughout the plans of the college" (*Report on the Phoenix College 1989/1990 Strategic Planning Process*, 1989, p. 2).

Enrollment concerns were partially addressed through renewed outreach to K–12 students and to the community in general, marketing, and a reenergized business and industry training operation. The effect of those efforts, which are ongoing, is a significant slowing of enrollment decline in the difficult environment of a very strong economy coupled with a struggling feeder high school system.

The Maricopa Community Colleges were successful in passing a $386 million general bond election in November 1994. Phoenix College benefits from that bond election through the capacity to rebuild the campus plant infrastructure, update instructional and administrative equipment and technology, and remodel some of the older buildings and replace some buildings with new, modern buildings.

The campus climate issues, although clearly related systemically to the physical plant and enrollment concerns, were much more difficult to assess and even more difficult to affect. The 1990 college consultant elaborated on his appraisal of the risk-averse environment with discussion of the low level of trust and the depressed creativity within the organization. The consultant reported the perception of several interviewees that "parent-child" types of relationships were present between administration and faculty and also within administration itself (*Report on the Phoenix College 1989/1990 Strategic Planning Process*, 1989, p. 6).

Responding to dual forces of the technological society and the social concerns in urban centers is the essence of the mission of today's urban community college. Creating an environment that fosters that response in the place of the risk-averse environment described above is a most difficult challenge. The emerging literature of chaos theory and complexity (Stacey, 1996), agile organizations (Goldman, Nagel, and Preiss, 1995), and self-organizing systems (Wheatley, 1992) held important messages for the new Phoenix College administration in assisting the college in building on its strengths and moving forward to a more open, inclusive, and participatory climate in which innovation and creativity could flourish and the challenges of today's urban environment could be met.

Starting the Journey

The description of Phoenix College in the early 1990s as static, hierarchical, and paternalistic in relationships, lacking risk-taking behavior, maintaining the status quo, and suffering from a lack of trust (*Report on the Phoenix College 1989/1990 Strategic Planning Process*, 1989) is not unique among higher education institutions or organizations in general. The key question is, How does an organization move from an older, mechanistic model to a more adaptive, interactive one? Some might be tempted to pick through the institution for best practices and recommend those for emulation. Others might seek a template to place over the institution or a step-by-step process to fix problems. But all of these are efforts to change by external methods of control. Long-term change—"real" change—in the way individuals see themselves and others and in the planning and decision-making processes of the organization is an interactive process in itself.

How is this type of change facilitated? We suggest some behaviors to begin this ongoing journey:

- Identify values or broad guiding principles for the organization and the individuals in it.
- Create situations where collaborative interactions can occur among individuals and groups of individuals.
- Create an information-rich climate.
- Encourage risk-taking behavior.
- Develop processes for problem solving and decision making with few rules that only seek to guide the interactions.
- Work toward a culture that is safe and has reduced fear.

From Theory to Practice

Margaret Wheatley describes a newer model of well-ordered organizations in *Leadership and the New Science:* "We also create order when we invite conflicts and contradictions to rise to the surface, when we search them out, highlight them, even allowing them to grow large and worrisome. We need to support people in the hunt for unsettling or disconfirming information, and provide them with the resources of time, colleagues, and opportunities for processing the information. . . . We can encourage vital organizational ambiguity with plans that are open, visions that inspire but do not describe, and by the encouragement of questions that ask 'Why?' many times over" (1992, p. 116).

Phoenix College, like most large organizations, struggles with the ongoing need for communication in the midst of the danger of information overload. The president, consistent with the college and district culture, which relies heavily on internal e-mail, sends regular "Campus Updates" to all of the college faculty and staff through e-mail and invites questions and comments in response. College faculty and staff are also invited several times each year to open campus discussions on strategic topics such as enrollment, diversity, or major facility project development.

These campus discussions and the information gathered from them are part of the college planning processes that emerged through collaboration of the college planning council and the faculty senate. The college strategic objectives, facilities development, budget development, and departmental planning are all part of these planning processes. The North Central Association Evaluation Team in its 1996 visit reported, "There is no attempt to keep anything secret on the campus, and PC has used all the tools available to keep its constituencies informed at all times" (Commission on Institutions of Higher Education of the North Central Association of Colleges and Schools, 1996, p. 59).

The work of Process Improvement Teams to study important issues and units of the college has affirmed the benefit of participatory processes: "We know that the best way to build ownership is to give over the creative process to those who will be charged with its implementation. . . . It doesn't work to just ask people to sign on when they haven't been involved in the design process, when they haven't experienced the plan as a living, breathing thing" (Wheatley, 1992, p. 66).

At Phoenix College, Process Improvement Teams have studied areas as diverse as Custodial Services, Financial Aid, Instructional Support Services, and the migration from a Center for Teaching and Learning to a Technology and Development Department. In each case the Team was composed of faculty and staff from across the campus who had interest in the topic and who wanted to participate, including the involved department. The president meets with each team at its first meeting to discuss the general parameters and charge: What processes occur? How do they interact? What is working well? What might be improved? Teams have a facilitator and select their own team leader. At the conclusion of the deliberations, generally two to four months, the president meets again with the team to discuss findings and recommendations.

Recommendations from the Custodial Services Team resulted in custodial staff being included on the hiring committees for custodians and in a change to the contract under which some custodial services were performed. The Financial Aid Team's recommendations will result in a major remodeling of the Financial Aid Office in 1997. The Instructional Support Team's recommendations provided the framework for a major reorganization in instruction and vastly improved college processes. The almost year-long process that resulted in the creation of a new Technology and Development Department was, as is not uncommon, very painful at times and consumed a great amount of faculty and staff energy and time. The outcome has been an innovative and very active support department for the college, particularly with technological support for the faculty and staff. Additionally, there are collegewide discussion groups about technology and its effects on teaching and learning, informing the development of a college technology plan.

Program development is an important characteristic of the more open, less risk-averse environment. Certificate and degree programs are in various stages of development in areas as diverse as Tribal Court Advocacy, Therapeutic Massage, and Golf Course Operations. Significant program renovation is occurring in other areas such as Emergency Medical Technician, Food Service Operations, and Computer Information Systems. Each of these new or revised programs responds to Phoenix College's particular community needs, serving the very diverse social needs and preparing students for work in a technological society.

The Future

Some faculty discussions have centered on the necessity for increased responsibility and accountability as participation in decision-making processes increase. Faculty have commented on "how much work this is!" There are, of course, those among the faculty and staff who are not pleased with the direction of the college or who choose not to participate in the open planning and decision-making processes. However, the benefits of the infusion of principles of complexity theory and self-organization into the college culture and climate are both internal and external. A more creative, innovative climate fosters program development and community outreach that fulfills the community college mission toward those dual forces of the technological society and urban societal needs. Thus, the very dilemmas that Phoenix College is faced with has become a source of potential. The diverse population and the necessary access to information that the technological world requires and affords become an asset to the interactive organization that Phoenix College seeks to become.

Formidable challenges still exist for the college now and in the future. Maintaining a steady enrollment in the midst of a very strong economy in the urban setting requires concentrated effort and continual program development. A recent community assessment indicates that local business awareness of college-provided training programs must be strengthened. At the same time, internal "turf battles" and competition for resources between departments could impede program development. Perhaps the most prominent internal need is for ongoing, energetic communication to facilitate identifying and affirming common college goals and direction and strengthening trust within the organization. The college commitment to open processes, collegewide forums and discussions, and participatory processes such as Process Improvement Teams will all assist Phoenix College in meeting its future successfully and serving its urban communities.

References

Boyer, E. (ed). *Building Communities: A Vision for a New Century.* Washington, D.C.: American Association of Community Colleges, 1988.

Commission on Institutions of Higher Education of the North Central Association of Colleges and Schools. *Report of a Visit to Phoenix College.* Phoenix: Commission on Institutions of Higher Education of the North Central Association of Colleges and Schools, 1996.

Elliott, P. G. *The Urban Campus: Educating the New Majority for the New Century.* Phoenix: Oryx Press, 1994.

Goldman, S. L., Nagel, R. N. and Preiss, K. *Agile Competitors and Virtual Organizations.* San Francisco: Van Nostrand Reinhold, 1995.

Padgett, M. "Central Phoenix Shows Signs of Decline." *Arizona Republic,* Nov. 18, 1994, p. B3.

Report on the Phoenix College 1989/1990 Strategic Planning Process. Phoenix: Great Visions, Inc., 1989.

Senge, P. M. *The Fifth Discipline: The Art and Practice of the Learning Organization.* New York: Currency Doubleday, 1990.

Sidwell, R. "'Tis All in Peeces, All Cohaerence Gone." *Holistic Education Review,* winter 1990, pp. 28–32.

Stacey, R. D. *Complexity and Creativity in Organizations.* San Francisco: Berrett-Koehler Publishers, 1996.

Waldrop, M. M. *Complexity.* New York: Touchstone, 1992.

Wheatley, M. J. *Leadership and the New Science: Learning About Organization from an Orderly Universe.* San Francisco: Berrett-Koehler, 1992.

Zohar, D., and Marshall, I. *The Quantum Society.* New York: Quill, 1994.

J. MARIE PEPICELLO is president of Phoenix College, Arizona.

MARSHA HOPKINS is a faculty member at Phoenix College, Arizona.

Community colleges can serve as agents of change to improve women's condition if their leaders desire. Current literature on organizational change and leadership in the community college is examined from three feminist perspectives as one means to assess this desire.

A Feminist Critique of Organizational Change in the Community College

Barbara K. Townsend, Susan B. Twombly

Feminists believe that organizational change is central to improving the condition of women. Without change, women's social, political, and economic conditions will continue to be unequal to men's, and women will not have a significant voice in the power structures that drive society. Moreover, because traditionally organizations have been led and dominated by men (and community colleges are no exception), organizational change will not occur unless it is specifically planned and supported by organizational leaders.

The kind of change that feminists envision is not mere tinkering but requires a paradigmatic shift, a breaking out of the mold of patriarchal thinking. Levy and Merry's (1986) distinction between first-order and second-order changes in organizations helps us understand the kind of change feminists consider necessary. First-order changes are those relatively minor adjustments that leave the organization's core essentially intact and that occur naturally as a system grows and matures. In contrast, second-order changes are "multidimensional, multi-level, qualitative, discontinuous, radical organizational change[s] involving a paradigmatic shift" (p. 5). The assumption underlying this concept of second-order change is that organizations, as social systems, have a worldview consisting of high-level abstract beliefs that shape organizational purpose, policies, structure, and practices (p. 10). Thus, in order to effect second-order or fundamental change in organizations, its worldview—the organizational philosophy, beliefs, values, structure, policies, operations, and often unconscious presuppositions—must change.

Levy and Merry's perspective is consistent with that of Gareth Morgan (1986), who argues that the image or the metaphor used to describe organizations shapes how we look at them. One of the metaphors he uses, that of the psychic prison, is particularly relevant for this chapter. If we see organizations as creations of the psyche, argues Morgan, we run the risk of becoming imprisoned or confined by the very images, ideas, and thoughts that create the organization. Feminists view organizations as creations of a patriarchal psyche, which operates as a conceptual prison, producing and reproducing organizational purpose, policies, structures, and practices that give dominance to male values. Psychic prisons carry the possibilities of their own transformation and change through self-reflection and a search for hidden meaning, a form of organizational psychotherapy. However, transformation becomes more difficult when it is in the interests of groups to promote one pattern of belief rather than another (p. 230).

The concepts of psychic prisons and second-order, paradigmatic change are a far cry from the vision of rational, planned change frequently advocated for higher education institutions. These more complex understandings of organizations and of change itself are necessary in order to bring about the kinds of changes advocated by feminists. Without leaders attempting paradigmatic shifts to alter the culture and practices of organizations, most feminists believe that change will not occur in male-dominated organizations. Certainly the experience of the past two decades suggests that merely increasing the number of women in leadership positions does not by itself bring about institutional change.

In this chapter we will examine some current (1990s) thinking about organizational change and leadership in community colleges to determine to what extent the thinking addresses the need for the community college to be an agent of change for the women in it. Since there are varying positions about what needs to be done to alter gender relations, the literature will also be assessed for which feminist perspectives are reflected in it.

Possible Feminist Agendas for the Community College

Whereas all feminists agree on the necessity of change because organizations are inherently patriarchal and benefit men more than women, several different approaches to change can be identified in contemporary feminism. The approaches differ in the extent to which they reflect second-order or paradigmatic changes considered necessary to restructure organizations for the benefit of women. From among a variety of feminist perspectives, we have selected three major ones: liberal, socialist, and cultural feminism. At the risk of oversimplifying, we will outline very briefly some of the differences among these three perspectives.

Liberal Feminists. The liberal feminist agenda has as its main objective securing equal opportunities for women and men. Generally speaking, liberal feminists desire to identify and remove barriers to women's equal participation and achievement. These barriers tend to have three conceptual bases: equal opportunities (or lack thereof), sex role socialization, and sex stereotyping and sex discrimination (Acker, 1994). Much of the higher education literature written about women has taken a liberal feminist approach. Strategies for change usually focus on the socialization process, attempt to change attitudes, and use formal policies and legal channels (Acker, 1994). Thus advocates for change in the community college might include the following in their agenda: equal pay for equal work, equal access to high-level positions, affirmative action in hiring, establishment and enforcement of sexual harassment policies, provision of child care facilities, establishment and use of a gender-inclusive language policy, and establishment of paid maternity and other family leave policies. Most of the items on the liberal feminist agenda have received at least some attention in many community colleges, partly because the national mood of the country during the 1970s and 1980s was sensitive to such issues as sexual harassment, salary inequities, and family leave policies.

Liberal feminists helped bring to the general public's consciousness the patriarchal thinking and behavior that necessitated a liberal feminist agenda. Regrettably, the achievement of most items on their agenda has not led to second-order organizational change. Rather, liberal feminists' proposed changes can be viewed as basically first-order changes, adjustments that may still leave intact an organization's patriarchal core.

Cultural Feminists. We have chosen cultural feminism, as opposed to radical or post-structural feminism, as the second feminist lens because of its influence on community college leaders in particular. Drawing from the work of Carol Gilligan's *In a Different Voice* (1982) and Belenky, Clinchy, Goldberger, and Tarule's *Women's Ways of Knowing* (1986), cultural feminists believe that women learn, communicate, and lead differently than men. Cultural feminists advocate strategies such as incorporating feminist pedagogy in the classroom, implementing women's studies programs, emphasizing women's ways of knowing, advocating specific leadership training programs for women, and changing the operation and nature of the organization to be more accommodating to women's leadership, learning, and communication styles. By their valuing of the essential differences between men and women, these strategies reflect a paradigmatic shift from liberal feminism, which basically advocates changes that will enable women to compete more effectively in a patriarchal society.

If all the items on the cultural feminists' agenda were implemented in educational organizations, second-order change might indeed result. However, the extent of community colleges' attention to items on the cultural feminist agenda is not known. The limited evidence is primarily about women's studies and leadership training programs for women. As of 1996, women's studies programs exist in only fifteen two-year schools (Peterson's Guide to Two-Year Schools, 1997). Also, over three thousand women administrators in the community colleges have participated in the National Institute for Leadership Development, which espouses gender differences in leadership.

Socialist Feminists. Focusing on capitalism as the root cause of inequalities, socialist feminists have an agenda that clearly leads to second-order change. The long-term goal is to eliminate gender oppression; the immediate task is to lay bare the process by which oppression works, which is capitalism

(Acker, 1994). Most socialist feminists focus on reproduction of class, race, and gender inequities and on the role of institutions such as schools in this reproduction. This approach (although not with a feminist orientation) has been a popular one among critics of the community college (such as Dougherty, 1995; Karabel, 1972; Pincus, 1980; Zwerling, 1976). Focusing on class rather than gender, these authors have demonstrated how community colleges, rather than leading to massive upward mobility for lower-class students, have essentially reinforced the existing social class structure inherent in capitalism.

After laying bare the oppression caused by a capitalistic society, socialist feminists hope to achieve a different economic order that would result in fundamental structural change at all levels. Part of this change would include transformed gender relations so that women would no longer be economically, socially, and politically disadvantaged or oppressed. Having socialism rather than capitalism as the undergirding worldview for organizations clearly constitutes second-order change. However, society itself would have to undergo this same second-order change before it would become a reality in colleges.

Current Thinking About Organizational Change and Leadership

Levin (1994) notes how the community college change literature more often focuses on how societal and economic changes have influenced the institutions than on how community colleges have changed society. We found that most of the works we examined did not propose paradigmatic institutional change to improve women's or minorities' position in society. Rather, they tended to focus on change per se. For example, Raisman (1994) urges leaders to be proactive rather than reactive in the change process. Why? Because "those who do not direct a planned process of change may become enmeshed in changes they have not chosen" (p. 23). Other authors, such as Kesler, Perry, and Shay (1996) and Brennan, Mugleston, and Perdue (1996) write about why people resist change and how to overcome that resistance. Implicit in these works are the assumptions that planned change is desirable and leaders plan change.

Some of the change literature focuses on change to improve the position of the community college in the marketplace. Thus Alfred and Carter (1996) urge community college leaders to stop "tinkering" and commit to "fundamental change" (p. 14). The impetus for this change is the need to remain competitive in the postsecondary market.

Occasionally, change is advocated to enhance the community college's role in improving society, including gender and race relations. Thus Lorenzo and LeCroy (1994) argue for "fundamental change" in community colleges so that they may "meet more precisely the emerging expectations, attitudes, and conditions of the Information Age" (p. 1). Noting the country's pressing economic problems and such problems as crime, drugs, and lack of employment, the authors believe that the community college's "overall goal . . . [is] to create a culture of responsiveness that more clearly relates its comprehensive mission to these new societal circumstances" (p. 6), which include "growing demands to cultivate higher quality interactions based on race, ethnicity, sex, and class" (p. 19). Therefore, Lorenzo and LeCroy urge leaders to insist that the institution admit and employ underrepresented groups.

Rhoads and Valadez (1996) come the closest to presenting a vision of second-order change for community colleges, although they do not specifically write about women students, faculty, and administrators. Their vision welcomes difference in a setting characterized by "difference, complexity, and process" (p. 192). The authors propose critical multiculturalism and participatory democracy as "substantive involvement in organizational decision making" (p. 193) for all members of the community.

Based on case studies of several community colleges, Rhoads and Valdadez (1996) develop a portrait of a fictional ideal and democratic community college. This ideal college is characterized by inclusionary and collaborative administrative processes and a campus climate in which debate and conflict are viewed as essential to an empowered citizenry. There is equality for all, and issues of race, class, gender, and sexual orientation are at center stage. The authors conclude with principles to guide students, faculty, and administrators "concerned with restructuring more democratic and multicultural academic communities" (p. 210).

Several of these principles are relevant here. Their first principle argues for promoting "greater collaboration and more participatory management processes" (p. 210). The second "requires that community college officials create opportunities for others to assume leadership" (p. 210). Third, there should be a culturally diverse faculty, staff, and student body participating in organizational decision making (p. 210). And finally, one principle states that democratic community colleges embrace change as a way of life (p. 214).

Although Rhoads and Valadez employ the rhetoric of democracy and critical multiculturalism, the place of women in their vision is unclear. Women are included primarily as part of the current mantra of "race, class, and gender." Concern for gender thus potentially takes a back seat to issues of race and ethnicity or becomes submerged in a trendy nod to concerns of outsider groups. Additionally, if one accepts the idea that women are less likely to thrive in highly conflictual settings, then Rhoads and Valadez's conception of democratic community colleges as places thriving on conflict and debate may actually be at cross purposes with women's preferences for collaboration and connection.

Community College Leadership. In the works specifically addressing community college leadership, the authors typically do not speak of paradigmatic shifts to advance a multicultural, gender-inclusive organization. Instead, leaders are urged to focus their efforts on improving the community college's position with "customers" and "competitors" through such approaches as Total Quality Management (Alfred and Carter, 1993; Hudgins, Oliver, and Williams, 1993). Sometimes the focus is on leadership to improve learning (Baker and Associates, 1992; Myran, Zeiss, and Howdyshell, 1995).

This attention to efficiency and effectiveness and to processes such as Total Quality Management (TQM) appear on the surface to be gender neutral. However, as Bensimon (1995) has shown, the central postulates of TQM—that quality is defined by the customer, that quality is the reduction of variation, and that quality must be measurable—have patriarchal bases in modernism. As a result, TQM values conformity over difference. From this perspective, TQM and similar quality initiatives are inherently threatening to efforts to make colleges multicultural and gender inclusive (p. 608).

Most recent works on community college leadership do advocate changing the nature of governance and decision making in a way that suggests concepts proposed by Gilligan (1982) and Belenky, Clinchy, Goldberger, and Tarule (1986) about women's nature. For example, Baker and Associates (1992) argue that "a holistic, cultural approach to leading and managing community colleges is necessary" (p. ix). According to Baker and Associates, "Leaders shape behavior in others by . . . coaching, teaching, and role modeling" (p. x). In a later book, Baker (1994) outlines the tasks of twenty-first-century leadership as follows: "(1) boundary spanning, not defending, (2) empowering people, not controlling them, (3) working cooperatively, not competitively, (4) focusing on process, not product, (5) organizational flexibility, not product, (6) quality, not quantity, (7) sharing information, not guarding it, and (8) creativity or intuition, not primarily rationality" (p. xvi).

Although these tasks are potentially gender inclusive, advocacy of them without reference to gender issues suggests that men have appropriated these new ways of organizing without acknowledging or perhaps understanding that these are "women's ways." It is intriguing that feminist perspectives have possibly influenced thought about community college leadership but frustrating if and when this influence is not acknowledged.

In her study of the leadership agendas of five women community college presidents, Mott (1997) views feminist leadership as both process and content (pp. 50–51). Implicit in a feminist leadership process is sharing of power through such activities as collective decision making, "public rather than private problem solving," and "open communication" (p. 51). A feminist leadership agenda would include content or issues that address women's needs as well as men's, with an understanding that women's needs may be different from men's. For example, women students may be more concerned about an institution's resources for child care and physical safety on campus than are men students. As indicated above, it is now fashionable to encourage a leadership style that includes many of the dimensions of a feminist leadership process (for example, Baker and Associates, 1992). What Mott helps us see is that a feminist process is not enough to improve women's situation in the community college. If leadership is to improve women's condition in the community college, the leadership must have a content or agenda that includes attention to women's issues and needs.

Like Mott, Burgos-Sasscer (1993) is direct and forceful in her espousal of organizational change to improve the position of women (and minorities).

Implicitly, she includes both feminist process and content in the fourteen approaches to bring about the necessary change. Some approaches reflect the content of a liberal feminist agenda, for example, elimination of salary inequities between men and women and development of policies that deal with family needs. Other approaches suggest a cultural feminist perspective, for example, seminars on work style differences. Her vision has elements of second-order change in its insistence on the implicit value and worth of women and minorities in organizations.

Traces of this vision are also seen in the monograph *Beyond the Vision* (Simpson and others, 1993), which reports on grant-funded projects to diversify community college leadership in ten institutions. The two reports whose titles indicate a focus on change (Simpson, 1993; Hunter, 1993) reflect a liberal, feminist agenda. Simpson (1993) writes about efforts to recruit women and people of color into leadership positions. Hunter (1993) mentions the hiring of one woman as increasing the diversity of the leadership team. She also notes that a half-day session on sexual harassment was held for administrators and professional staff. Two other reports in this monograph reflect a cultural feminist perspective: they speak of workshops on gender team building (Grossbach, 1993) and gender differences (Nanke, 1993). Each of these workshops was conducted by Carolyn Desjardins, executive director of the National Institute for Leadership Development, which espouses gender differences in leadership.

Conclusion

We draw several conclusions from our review of current mainstream literature on community college organizational change and leadership. At the most basic level, the literature reflects little attention to feminist concerns. Although some gains have been made for women in community colleges and in the broader society, women's issues have ceased to receive the attention that they did in the 1970s and 1980s (Twombly 1993).

Next, it is unlikely that any feminist perspective other than liberal feminism or cultural feminism will be adopted at most community colleges. When we view current writings about community college organizational change and leadership through the various feminist agendas described above, we see few reflecting major paradigmatic shifts or second-order changes. Certainly, none reflect a socialist feminist perspective. That is, none critique the community college's role in perpetuating gender inequities and the consequent need to restructure the institution dramatically to avoid this perpetuation. The lack of a socialist feminist perspective is not surprising. Those who are committed to leadership in the community college and view them as mainstream organizations implicitly accept them as agents of capitalism and do not look to alter their economic function or role. Some works do reflect a liberal feminist perspective or a combination of liberal feminism and cultural feminism. Additionally, some people espouse what could be described as a cultural feminist style of leadership but not necessarily the implementation of a feminist agenda.

Finally, our review of the current, high-profile organizational change and leadership literature suggests two major rationales for organizational change: change to make community colleges more efficient and effective organizations, and change for democracy and critical multiculturalism. Although the two rationales are different, each seems to use the same approach to change. Both talk of changing the decision-making process to make it more inclusive and collaborative. In its adoption of inclusionary models of leadership for change, the change and leadership literature incorporates aspects of leadership promoted widely by feminists such as Cross and Ravekes (1990). Regrettably from a feminist perspective, this same literature offers few analyses of how women are affected by change and still fewer recommendations for even liberal reforms such as child care to help women students.

References

Acker, S. *Gendered Education*. Philadelphia: Open University Press, 1994.
Alfred, R. L., and Carter, P. (eds.) *Changing Managerial Imperatives*. New Directions for Community Colleges, no. 84. San Francisco: Jossey-Bass, 1993.
Alfred, R. L., and Carter, P. "Inside Track to the Future: Structures, Strategies, and Leadership for Change." *Community College Journal*, Feb.–Mar. 1996, pp. 10–19.
Baker, G. A., III (ed.). *A Handbook on the Community College in America: Its History, Mission, and Management*. Westport, Conn.: Greenwood Press, 1994. (ED 364 283)
Baker, G.A., III, and Associates. *Cultural Leadership: Inside America's Community Colleges*. Washington, D.C.: American Association of Community and Junior Colleges, 1992. (ED 350 049)
Belenky, M. F., Clinchy, B. M., Goldberger, N. R., and Tarule, J. M. *Women's Ways of Knowing*. New York: Basic Books, 1986.
Bensimon, E. "Total Quality Management in the Academy: A Rebellious Reading." *Harvard Educational Review*, 1995, 65 (4), 593–611.
Brennan, E., Mugleston, W., and Perdue, J. "When a Whole College Changes: Overcoming Inertia, Motivating Veteran Faculty and Staff." In *Proceedings of the Annual International Conference of the National Community College Chair Academy*. Phoenix: National Community College Chair Academy, 1996.
Burgos-Sasscer, R. "New Players in Management." In R. L. Alfred and P. Carter (eds.), *Changing Managerial Imperatives*. New Directions for Community Colleges, no. 84. San Francisco: Jossey-Bass, 1993.
Cross, C., and Ravekes, J. "Perceptions of Gender Discrimination: A Community College Case Study." *Journal of the American Association of Women Community and Junior Colleges*, 1990, 7–14.
Dougherty, K. *The Contradictory College: The Conflicting Origins, Impacts and Futures of the Community College*. Albany: State University of New York Press, 1995.
Gilligan, C. *In A Different Voice*. Boston: Harvard University Press, 1982.
Grossbach, S. "Hennepin Technical College: Leadership for Alliances." In M. Simpson and others (eds.), *Beyond the Vision: Implementation Strategies for Diversifying Community College Leadership*. Omaha, Nebr.: Metropolitan Community College Clearinghouse for Exemplary Practices in Leadership Diversity, 1993.
Hudgins, J., Oliver, S., and Williams, S. K. "Students First! Reconceptualizing Support Services." In R. L. Alfred and P. Carter (eds.), *Changing Managerial Imperatives*. New Directions for Community Colleges, no. 84. San Francisco: Jossey-Bass, 1993.
Hunter, M. J. "On the Threshold of Change: Leadership Diversity at Western Nebraska Community College." In M. Simpson and others (eds.), *Beyond the Vision: Implementation*

Strategies for Diversifying Community College Leadership. Omaha, Nebr.: Metropolitan Community College Clearinghouse for Exemplary Practices in Leadership Diversity, 1993.

Karabel, J. "Community Colleges and Social Stratification." *Harvard Educational Review,* 1972, *42* (4), 521–562.

Kesler, R., Perry, C., and Shay, G. "So They Are Resistant to Change: Strategies for Moving an Immovable Object." Proceedings of the annual international conference of the National Community College Chair Academy, Phoenix, Ariz., 1996.

Levin, J. "Community Colleges as Organizations of Change." Paper presented at annual meeting of Association for the Study of Higher Education, Tucson, Ariz., 1994.

Levy, A., and Merry, U. *Organizational Transformation: Approaches, Strategies, and Theories.* New York: Praeger, 1986.

Lorenzo, A. L., and LeCroy, N. A. "A Framework for Fundamental Change in the Community College: Creating a Culture of Responsiveness." Warren, Mich.: Institute for Future Studies, Macomb Community College, 1994.

Morgan, G. *Images of Organizations.* Beverly Hills, Calif.: Sage Publications, 1986.

Mott, M. C. "Women Community College Presidents' Leadership Agendas." Unpublished doctoral dissertation, Center for the Study of Higher Education, University of Arizona, 1997.

Myran, G., Zeiss, T., and Howdyshell, L. *Community Colleges in the New Century: Learning to Improve Learning.* Washington, D.C.: American Association of Community Colleges, 1995.

Nanke, L. "Cultural Diversity Awareness and Sensitivity at Kirkwood Community College." In M. Simpson and others (eds.), *Beyond the Vision: Implementation Strategies for Diversifying Community College Leadership.* Omaha, Nebr.: Metropolitan Community College Clearinghouse for Exemplary Practices in Leadership Diversity, 1993.

Peterson's Guide to Two-Year Schools. [http://www.petersons.com/ugrad/select/u24290se.html]. Apr. 26, 1997.

Pincus, F. "The False Promise of Community Colleges: Class Conflict and Vocational Education." *Harvard Educational Review,* 1980, *50* (3), 332–361.

Raisman, N. "Plan for Change Before Someone Else Plans It for You." *Trusteeship,* 1994, *2* (4), 23–26.

Rhoads, R., and Valadez, J. R. *Democracy, Multiculturalism, and the Community College: A Critical Perspective.* New York: Garland Publishing, 1996.

Simpson, M. "Collaborative Change: A Consortium Approach to Leadership Diversity." In M. Simpson and others (eds.), *Beyond the Vision: Implementation Strategies for Diversifying Community College Leadership.* Omaha, Nebr.: Metropolitan Community College Clearinghouse for Exemplary Practices in Leadership Diversity, 1993.

Twombly, S. "What We Know About Women in Community Colleges: An Examination of the Literature Using Feminist Phase Theory." *Journal of Higher Education,* 1993, *64* (2), 186–210.

Zwerling, S. *Second Best: The Crisis of the Community College.* New York: McGraw-Hill, 1976.

Barbara K. Townsend is professor in the Department of Leadership at The University of Memphis and a former community college faculty member and administrator.

Susan B. Twombly is associate professor in the Department of Teaching and Learning at the University of Kansas.

Like most contemporary organizations, community colleges are faced with the transition to a new postmodern era, requiring clear mission to match diffuse boundaries and greater thoughtfulness about growth and measurement to match new challenges of organizational fragmentation and inconsistency.

The Postmodern Challenge: Changing Our Community Colleges

William Bergquist

The shift from a modern to a postmodern social structure is founded on technology and information (Drucker, 1989; Jameson, 1991). Many contemporary organizations are going through major transformations, becoming increasingly complex and variable systems that must respond to an unpredictable and turbulent environment and economy (Bergquist, 1993).

The challenge for contemporary community colleges is one of understanding and fully appreciating both the problems and potentials associated with shifts both from premodern to modern and from modern to postmodern in our communities, nation, and world. Surprisingly, American higher educational institutions in general and community colleges in particular have often chosen to remain rather ignorant of these profound societal changes (Bloland, 1995).

The Premodern World: Simplicity and Tradition

We may be entering a postmodern era, but our sight is as much backward as it is forward. We look back with a distorted and often nostalgic perspective on a world of strong community college leaders who could decisively solve straightforward problems and of faculty, administrators, and staff who found gratification in the work they performed and the community they served. Typically, our colleges were established in communities that had an identity or at least homogeneity regarding values, culture, or socioeconomic status. Even in urban settings, our community colleges were often created to serve a distinct community group or need.

Given the pressures under which we live in our postmodern world, it is quite understandable that we might wish for a simpler place and time. Yet there is also realism in our search for the premodern world. First, the premodern still exists in our society. A thin veneer of modernism covers the fundamental and deeply rooted premodernism of virtually all societies. This is a central message in postmodernism: a successful postmodern organization will inevitably incorporate diverse elements from many times and places. The premodern world is also of great relevance because it holds at least partial answers for our emerging postmodern world. The premodern world can help us set the agenda for our colleges with regard to reemerging values. It also provides us with important insights about the human enterprise. Community colleges situated in an emerging postmodern world are likely to be successful, in part, if they borrow from both the premodern and modern worlds while also inventing new forms and formulating new perspectives that are neither premodern nor modern.

The Modern World: Giants and Managers

Large organizations represent the pinnacle of modernism in most societies. Modern organizations speak a common language. They look alike and operate in the same manner. A human service executive in France can understand the financial statement of a Taiwanese hospital, just as the manager of marketing in a South American company can understand the strategies used by a corporate planner in India. The languages of nations may differ, but the language of modern organizations is universal. Instead of the distinctive vernacular (ritual, stories, customs) of premodern organizations, we live with the universality of modernism.

The primary objective of modern organizations is to become and stay large. Whereas premodern organizations concentrated on organizational continuity and tradition (which usually required very gradual growth), modern organizations emphasize rapid growth. As modern organizations expand in size and add more units and levels of organizational structure to accommodate their growth, organizations become more difficult to control. Although the premodern culture of an organization provides some integration through its customs, dress, ritual, and stories of great triumphs and defeats, this premodern glue is often disparaged in most modern organizations. Furthermore, this culture does not offer sufficient integration for very large organizations. As organizations grow more complex in the modern world, increasing attention must be given to those activities that enhance coordination and cooperation among the differentiated functions of the organization.

As organizations become larger or older, they also require clearer boundaries so that leaders can maintain control. Financial monitoring and auditing functions are added. Personnel offices ensure uniformity of hiring practices as well as coordinating training efforts. Newsletters proliferate, as do office managers, purchasing agents, and departmental administrators. These offices, roles, and management functions are devoted to the integrative functions of the organization. As the organization grows larger and older, an increasingly large proportion of the resources of the organization must be devoted to these integrative functions (Bergquist, 1993). As a result, modern organizations that are large or old are likely to become less efficient. Unless they control the marketplace, these larger or older organizations may be unable to compete with those that are smaller or younger.

There is decreasing clarity and consistency in the mission and purpose of modern organizations. In general, mission statements have been created primarily for public image and marketing, or, in the case of private institutions, the mission is directed simply to the "bottom line." In contrast with the visible and clear boundaries of modern organizations, mission statements do not provide much clarity or guidance for those who work in or evaluate these institutions. Whereas the premodern world is built on land and reputation, with a strong parallel emphasis on service and community, the modern world is built on a different form of capital: money. In a modern world that values democratic ideals and fosters the expectation or myth of upward social mobility, new wealth and a more transient bourgeoisie are dominant.

In essence, the modern world has produced a shift from direct sources of personal meaning in life through one's work and one's family to indirect sources, such as wealth and consumption. The premodern man or woman takes pride in the cultivation of crops or production of crafts, and in the raising of a family and provision of food and shelter to members of the family. By contrast, modern workers are often alienated from the products of their work and from ownership for the means of production (Jameson, 1991). Alienation from the direct sources of meaning in our work is joined with the alienation that comes from the loss of personal voice and influence, and with the loss of interdependency among people who once worked together in premodern communities.

The Postmodern World: Fragmentation and Complexity

As we enter the postmodern era, it appears that the integrative services of the modern era—even if extensive—often are not sufficient to hold the organization together. Even with greater attention given to organizational culture and to creating a strong feeling of solidarity, contemporary organizations are experiencing pervasive fragmentation, chaos, and inconsistency. One part of the organization does not know or care what the other parts are doing. Growing frustration is founded on frequent and counterproductive reorganizations. Conglomerations of differing structures always seem to be "in planning." Divisions fail to coordinate their efforts with other divisions. Clearly established organizationwide priorities are nowhere to be found. A general sense of foreboding or panic, postmodern "edginess," pervades the organization.

Increasingly, two major questions must be asked by leaders with regard to these postmodern conditions. First, what is the right size for this particular organization or this particular unit of the organization? The integration of functions in large-scale organizations may no longer be possible, or, if it is possible, it requires much too large a proportion of the total resources of the organization for this organization to survive. Administrative costs tend to rise, not fall, with expansion in the size and complexity of collegiate organizations (Leslie and Rhoades, 1995, p. 195). Effective postmodern leaders speak about appropriate size rather than indiscriminate growth.

The second major question that postmodern leaders must ask concerns the nature of the integration that does occur. Traditionally, integration has been equated with control. We keep organizations from flying apart by ensuring that all operations of the organization are tightly controlled. In the modern world, this means that organizations will be structured hierarchically, with each person receiving orders from someone situated immediately above him or her in this hierarchy. An alternative way to think of integration emphasizes influence instead of control. Rather than using the formal hierarchy of the organization, successful postmodern leaders use more informal and powerful channels of communication and leadership by example (Heifetz, 1994; Kanter, 1983; Wheatley, 1992). Rather than looking to the hierarchy to gain control, they look to the network and the web to exert influence. Key people and groups located at nodal points often play a much greater role in bringing about integration than do those at the top of the organization.

We are discovering that both the size and the shape of most modern organizations fit poorly with the emerging postmodern conditions of our society. The traditional vertical structure of modern organizations is called into question. With the introduction of high-speed interconnecting communication technologies there is no longer the need for trickle-down communication. The new knowledge workers are no longer willing to work for a boss who closely monitors and supervises their work. Reengineering has taught us that modern administrators too often remanage processes that have already been engaged at a lower level of the organization. In the near future, community colleges will, like other postmodern organizations, move away from vertical control to cross-functional teams and complex reporting relationships (Johnson, 1997; Myran, Zeiss, and Howdyshell, 1996).

Acknowledging Fragmentation and Inconsistency

Contemporary community colleges resemble other postmodern organizations in that they are often both complex and fragmented. Premodern, modern, and postmodern structures, processes, and procedures in these colleges intermingle. We find premodern elements in the celebrations, ceremonies, and retreats that bring members of a community college together for recognition and reflection. The powerful role played by these elements of organizational culture is only now fully appreciated among community college leaders (Bergquist, 1992; Johnson, 1997). Examples of the intermingling of modern and postmodern are even more prevalent. Many community colleges exist as both independent, autonomous institutions that are characteristically modern, and as interdependent collaborating members of complex consortia and partnerships that are notably postmodern (Roueche, Taber, and Roueche, 1995). These new organizational forms are created to allow for the expansion of resources through interinstitutional cooperation rather than the independent growth of each individual institution (Bergquist, Betwee, and Meuel, 1995).

Hollow organizations are created to bring together autonomous institutions and agencies to provide educational services over a relatively long duration. These organizations have little centralized control, relying instead on a clear mission and carefully crafted cooperative agreements. The services provided by a hollow organization are not typically independently available to any one community college. The League for Innovation has been bringing together community colleges for many years to share resources. The league recently established partnerships between community colleges and corporations to sponsor conferences, disseminate information, and conduct special projects, thereby further broadening the scope of this cooperative venture. The National Workforce Development Study offers another example of a hollow postmodern alliance (Zeiss and Assoc., 1997). This national study is a product of cooperation between several national associations and brings together information for workforce training and development from both community college administrators and employers of community college graduates.

Virtual organizations are similarly formed among several community colleges to respond to short-term student or community needs that cannot be met by any one college. Virtual organizations are more likely than hollow organizations to be coordinated by a single agency or institution, and they typically serve one specific function and disband when the need no longer exists. Many distance education programs function as virtual organizations, with one college serving as the central administrator for a distributed set of courses and learning sites (American Association of Community Colleges, 1997). Virtual organizations are likely to become even more common with the movement of many governmental funds from national to local levels. Shreve (1996), for example, predicts that recent reforms in welfare, health care, and workforce development are likely to lead community colleges to consolidate services and establish virtual partnerships with other community agencies. They will form these alliances to obtain block grants based in state or community rather than federal funding. Community colleges are well positioned for these more locally focused funds, provided they work in conjunction with other institutions and agencies in the community.

The complexity of postmodern community colleges is also evident inside the organization. Ad hoc task forces exist in many contemporary colleges alongside modern bureaucracies. Small project teams are integrated with formal, hierarchically organized departments. Unique incentive programs and joint union-management problem-solving groups build on, yet also challenge, traditional organizational policies and procedures. Maricopa Community Colleges (Arizona) create intensive ad hoc planning groups to design and implement many of their new programs, making use, for example, of a think tank to drive their "Quantum Quality" initiatives (Assar, 1993).

Appreciating Scope and Measurement

The new problems facing contemporary community colleges result in part from their sheer size and the conflicting demands of various constituencies served by these organizations. Virtually all medium- to large-sized organizations in North America now find it hard to measure anything of importance, discover either the extent or scope of the problems they face, or determine whether or not the problem has even been solved (Gleick, 1987; Wheatley, 1992). The larger the institution, the more difficult becomes the problem of measurement and scale.

What about a large educational institution? From one perspective, a major community college such as Metropolitan (a fictitious institution) is a success, but from another perspective it is an impending disaster. Metro's balance sheet and financial reserves are impressive. Morale is high among alumni and executive staff. Other colleges in the area look weak and disorganized. Long-term financial projections, however, point to major losses. Personnel reports at Metro suggest slow-brewing labor problems. Demographic analyses reveal potential drops in student enrollments. Shifting community support and funding or a technological breakthrough may change the rules of the game drastically. Which perspective is valid? They are both correct. However, one report is likely to be sent by the president to the Metropolitan Board of Trustees and another to the executive officers of the college. Which report, if any, do the union leaders at Metro receive? We must learn to live with this ambiguity in measurement. This is part of the postmodern condition.

If we cannot even measure, let alone evaluate, what is happening in the organization, how can its leaders recognize current problems or know for certain that they have solved the organization's problems, let alone planned for its future? This profound question has not gone unnoticed by contemporary community college leaders. Some of these leaders respond by moving outside their institution to gain a broader perspective regarding the functioning of their institution. They turn to one of the major tools of Total Quality Management—benchmarking—to compare their own performance with that of other community colleges and related organizations (Johnson, 1997). The new technologies, as well as the flourishing of hollow organizations and other cooperative arrangements among postmodern institutions, make benchmarking a useful assessment tool for community colleges.

Other community college leaders have addressed the problem of measurement by challenging many of the established assumptions about assessment of organizational quality and effectiveness in educational institutions. Traditional input-based criteria of institutional quality are no longer adequate (Bergquist, 1995). These input measures focus exclusively on the extent and quality of resources in the college, such as number of faculty, degrees held by faculty, size of library, extent of instructional technology, and number of buildings. The complexity of contemporary colleges and the capacity for extensive sharing of resources between colleges and between the college and the community make the traditional enumeration of institutional resources no longer appropriate. Measurements must instead be taken of the educational outcomes produced by the college. These output-based criteria of quality tell us how effectively the college makes use of the resources that are available to it. This approach becomes even more potent when linked directly to institutional purposes and the strategic planning of the college. The key question is no longer, How do we gather more resources? The key question instead is, How do we more effectively achieve outcomes that match the purpose(s) of our college? (Midlands Technical College, 1997).

The postmodern community college may even want to move beyond an output- or outcome-based approach to quality and focus instead on the difference that the college makes in the life of its students. This value-added criterion of quality emphasizes the role of the community college as an agency for workforce development and community education. This value-added approach to community college quality focuses on learning rather than teaching, and on ways in which the college educates its most disadvantaged and "at-risk" students, as well as extending educational services to all members of the community (O'Banion, 1996). A college that takes pride in its successful achievement of specific outcomes may be deluding itself if these outcomes have been achieved through serving only the "best and brightest" learners or if these outcomes and the underlying purposes of the college are not responsive to the most fundamental needs of the community this college serves.

Articulating a Clear and Compelling Mission

The issue of mission is intensified in the postmodern world because the bottom line and continuing growth are no longer adequate criteria of performance for either public or private institutions (Drucker, 1989). Postmodern organizations need clear direction, given the ambiguity of their boundaries and the turbulence of the environments in which they operate (Bergquist, 1993). Postmodern organizations are usually the inverse of modern organizations with regard to mission and boundaries. They may have unclear or changing boundaries. They must have a clear and consistent mission. Such an inversion tends to counter our normal way of thinking. We are often inclined to construct firm boundaries when the world around us is turbulent and unpredictable.

Many community colleges will survive only if they operate from clearly articulated statements of mission that relate directly to the effects that the institution has on the lives of its students and other key stakeholders. A community college that defines a specific product or service as something needed by a specific constituency is more likely to be successful in our chaotic, postmodern world than a college that tries to appeal to a much broader audience with a variety of products or services that do not hold together in a coherent fashion. Furthermore, community colleges that have clearly defined and enacted missions, coupled with a compelling, shared vision, will tend to attract attention and commitment (Myran, Zeiss, and Howdyshell, 1996). Organizational mission and vision become *strange attractors* (Gleick, 1987) that focus the resources and energy of people working inside the organization, as well as those who support the organization.

In recent years, the emphasis on mission in community colleges has taken on even greater import and a specific focus with the introduction of continuous quality improvement (CQI) initiatives, an emphasis on the *learning organization* (Senge, 1990) and other related strategic approaches to institutional improvement. Although CQI and the learning organization have not lived up to their initial promise, the concepts of quality and continuous learning are now deeply embedded in the strategic thinking of numerous community college administrators and faculty members. With regard to the emphasis on quality, we are likely to find even greater support for this notion with the introduction of the new Malcolm Baldridge criteria for judging institutional quality in higher education (Malcolm Baldridge National Quality Award, 1995; Seymour, 1994). Similarly, the notion of organizational learning is likely to gain increasing momentum not only with the introduction of the Baldridge standards into community colleges but also with the new emphasis on *learning communities* and *learning colleges* in our two-year institutions (O'Banion, 1996, 1997).

Contemporary community colleges can choose to work from their mission and foster both learning and continuous improvement as a central feature in their culture. In adopting this strategy, a contemporary community college positions itself for a postmodern world in which organizations become increasingly flexible with regard to boundaries. These postmodern colleges can establish their own market niches and shift with the changing nature of the market while preserving a distinctive identity and purpose. They are likely to be much more open to changes in clientele and move across previously restrictive boundaries, such as product or service areas or even regional or national boundaries. In dropping their boundaries, postmodern colleges are likely to be more fully responsive to changing technologies, changing student and community needs, and changing sources of revenues.

The diffusion of boundaries in our postmodern world is found both between and within organizations. In the modern world, internal boundaries are clearly preserved. Employees communicate by memo or letter to supervisors and subordinates. In the postmodern organization, there is much less consistency in the flow of information throughout the organization. The postmodern world has returned to a premodern emphasis on informality (Bergquist, 1993). Rapid communication devices make the written word passé. The fax machine and e-mail are replacing memoranda and "snail" mail.

Boundaries between institutions have also become diffuse. Digitalized education has produced a revolution in the past decade that has led many community colleges to distribute educational programs over many media, including the Internet. "Virtual" colleges make use of courses created by instructors from many different kinds of organizations throughout the world (Gross, 1995). All 107 community colleges in California are presently upgrading their instructional technology in order to link with one another through a high-speed network ("On Line," 1997). With Internet videoconferencing, where does one of these colleges leave off and another one begin? How are the distinctive features of an individual California community college differentiated from the overall community college system in this state? And what is the community college role in international education? Nigel Paine (1996) poses the critical question: "Where does a community college fit in when a community is virtual and almost infinite?"

Even without electronic media, this is becoming an era in which traditional boundaries are shattered on a routine basis. College campuses are no longer sanctuaries for intellectual pursuits or isolated enclaves for middle-class white students (Bloland, 1995). Crime does not stop at the edge of campus, nor is a community college immune from the other social ills of its community. Some visionaries have suggested that community colleges should position themselves as "community building" institutions that link their own planning efforts with those of the community in which they reside (Harlacher and Gollattscheck, 1996). Community colleges have also been exposed for many years to the shattering of the boundaries between work and learning. Students commute to the campus, combining work and learning in their complex lives. Some community colleges have pushed even further by integrating the work and learning experience more fully, in some cases through new state and federal legislation (Bragg and Hamm, 1995). The community colleges in Minnesota merge with the four-year institutions and technical colleges (Healy, 1996). Throughout the United States and Canada new affiliations are formed between community colleges and four-year universities that yield innovative new career preparation programs in such diverse areas as technology management and health care administration.

Interpersonal boundaries have also been shattered. Oral, face-to-face communication is once again dominant with the emergence of short-term task forces and five-minute meetings. Many contemporary organizations provide a variety of permanent and temporary systems, yielding complex, mixed modes of organizational communication.

As a result of the pervasive diffusion of boundaries, we face confusion and complexity in our personal and professional lives as well as in our organizations (Anderson, 1990; Gergen, 1991). In many situations, we do not know if we are inside or outside the organization. Are we at work, at home, or on the road, given the proliferation of car phones, home computers, e-mail and home-based fax machines? Is the edginess of the community college instructor or dean in part a continuing confusion about what is work, what is home, and what is leisure? Is the time we save with our wonderful new devices time that we take away from our own lives and the lives of people with whom we do not work, such as our friends and family?

Managing the Intersect

We find that the diffusion of boundaries is particularly notable in the proliferation of *intersect* organizations (Boulding, 1973). These new organizations
blend features of both public and private institutions and may help solve long-
standing problems in our society. Yet these intersect organizations are also subject to troubling ambiguity. Many contemporary community colleges exemplify
the intersect organization. These organizations operate on behalf of the public
and receive tax revenues from local, state, and even federal sources. However,
these revenues are now in decline (*Community College Times,* 1997). With significant reductions in tax revenues, community colleges must now operate like
for-profit businesses. The percentage of revenues that come from sales, service,
private gifts, and contracts is increasing, while the percentage from federal and
state government is decreasing (Institute for Research on Higher Education,
1996).

The president of a community college in western Canada recently
reported that less that 45 percent of the revenues at his institution now come
from provincial appropriations. Major research universities have been running
this way for many years. Community colleges are now joining them. To offset
declining tax revenues, public community colleges charge higher tuition (Healy
and Schmidt, 1997). They also seek out donations, voluntary services, and
other forms of philanthropic support, usually through formation of a nonprofit
foundation affiliated with the college. Our Canadian president, like many of
his entrepreneurial colleagues at other community colleges, also actively markets a wide range of profitable services—from corporate training to automo-
tive repair—and obtains additional funds through leasing various college
facilities. What is the status of this Canadian community college? Is it public
or private? How can we call it public when more than 50 percent of its revenues come from sources other than tax dollars?

At the heart of the matter is a troubling question: "Who Owns Higher
Education?" (Lazerson, 1997). It is no longer a struggle between the trustees,
administration, and faculty. It now also concerns many other stakeholders—
including large multinational corporations that are not even primarily
beholden to any particular national interests (Bloland, 1995). Why should the
publicly elected or appointed board of trustees of a community college be the
primary governing body when it represents less than 50 percent of the total
revenues?

An even more basic question should be asked. How does one lead an
intersect organization while contending with several constituencies and competing values and visions for the organization? Intersect leaders must build a
consensus regarding mission among their diverse constituencies and governing boards. They need mediation and negotiation skills. These leaders will
rarely be able to make use of traditional decision-making or problem-solving
processes of a rational or linear nature. Intersect leaders must be able to nego-
tiate across traditional boundaries, as well as live with considerable ambiguity.

Conclusions

The challenges for contemporary community colleges operating in postmodern times are exceptional. On the one hand, change and novelty can be motivators. New conditions force people to think in new ways and break out of old thought patterns. On the other hand, change and the unique are frightening. Postmodern conditions require that we listen to the "other"—those who have resided outside the comfortable confines of our collegiate institutions (Bloland, 1995).

Given that our colleges are deeply embedded in the values, structures, and vocabulary of modern life, we are particularly vulnerable to the critiques of postmodernism and to the threats of radical change in an emerging postmodern world (Bloland, 1995). We become frightened when the old structures fall away and we are left standing alone, without a sustaining tradition and without predictability.

Our colleges must confront the new with wisdom, courage, and vision if they are to thrive in an emerging postmodern era. Leaders of these institutions must in turn be able to understand, appreciate, and live with the troubling ambiguity of this emerging condition.

References

"Alabama Board Proposes $102 Million in Education Cuts." *Community College Times: Online Edition,* Aug. 24, 1997. [AACC home page]. Available online: http://www.aacc.nche/edu

American Association of Community Colleges. *Teleconferencing Resources at U.S. Community Colleges.* Washington D.C.: American Association of Community Colleges, 1997.

Anderson, W. *Reality Isn't What It Used To Be.* San Francisco: HarperSanFrancisco, 1990.

Assar, K. E. "Phoenix: Quantum Quality at Maricopa." *Change,* May–June 1993, pp. 32–35.

Berquist, W. H. *The Four Cultures of the Academy.* San Francisco: Jossey-Bass, 1992.

Bergquist, W. H. *The Postmodern Organization: Mastering the Art of Irreversible Change.* San Francisco: Jossey-Bass, 1993.

Bergquist, W. H. *Quality Through Access, Access with Quality: The New Imperative for Higher Education.* San Francisco: Jossey-Bass, 1995.

Bergquist, W., Betwee, J., and Meuel, D. *Building Strategic Relationships: How to Extend Your Organization's Reach Through Partnerships, Alliances, and Joint Ventures.* San Francisco: Jossey-Bass, 1995.

Bloland, H. "Postmodernism and Higher Education." *Journal of Higher Education,* 1995, 66 (5), 521–557.

Boulding, K. "Intersects: The Peculiar Organizations." In K. Bursk and The Conference Board (eds.), *Challenge to Leadership: Managing in a Changing World.* New York: Free Press, 1973.

Bragg, D. D., and Hamm, R. E. "The Opportunities for 'School-to-Work:' A National Study of Work-Based Learning in U.S. Community Colleges." *Community College Journal,* 1995, 65 (7), 39–44.

Drucker, P. *The New Realities.* New York: HarperCollins, 1989.

Gergen, K. *The Saturated Self: Dilemmas of Identity in Contemporary Life.* New York: HarperCollins, 1991.

Gleick, J. *Chaos: Making a New Science.* New York: Viking Penguin, 1987.

Gross, R. "Defining the Future: The New Mandate for Distance Learning in the Twenty-First Century." *Community College Journal,* 1995, 66 (2), 28–33.

Harlacher, E., and Gollattscheck, J. *The Community-Building College: Leading the Way to Community Revitalization.* Washington, D.C.: American Association of Community Colleges, 1996.

Healy, P. "Minnesota Tackles the Possibilities and Problems of a Public-College Merger." *Chronicle of Higher Education,* Dec. 20, 1996, p. A23.

Healy, P., and Schmidt, P. "At Public Colleges, the Tuition Debate Is a Mix of Philosophy and Practicality." *Chronicle of Higher Education,* May 30, 1997, p. A17.

Heifetz, R. *Leadership Without Easy Answers.* Cambridge, Mass.: Harvard University Press, 1994.

Institute for Research on Higher Education. "Footing the Bill: The Shifting Burden of Higher Education Finance." *Change,* Sept.–Oct. 1996, pp. 49–52.

Jameson, F. *Postmodernism or the Cultural Logic of Late Capitalism.* Durham, N.C.: Duke University Press, 1991.

Johnson, S. L. "Community College Leadership in the Age of Technology." *Leadership Abstracts,* 1997, *10* (5).

Kanter, R. M. *The Change Masters.* New York: Simon and Schuster, 1983.

Lazerson, M. "Who Owns Higher Education?" *Change,* Mar.–Apr. 1997, pp. 10–15.

Leslie, L. L., and Rhoades, G. "Rising Administrative Costs." *Journal of Higher Education,* 1995, *66* (2), 187–212.

Malcolm Baldrige National Quality Award. *Education Pilot Criteria: 1995.* Gaithersburg, Md.: National Institute of Standards and Technology, 1995.

Midlands Technical College. *Managing Your Institution's Effectiveness: AACC Strategies and Solutions Series.* Washington, D.C.: American Association of Community Colleges, 1997.

Myran, G., Zeiss, T., and Howdyshell, L. "Community College Leadership in the New Century." *Leadership Abstracts,* 1996, *9* (2).

O'Banion, T. "Learning Communities, Learning Organizations, and Learning Colleges." *Leadership Abstracts,* 1996, *9* (8).

O'Banion, T. *A Learning College for the Twenty-First Century.* Washington, D.C.: American Council on Education, American Association of Community Colleges, and Oryx Press, 1997.

"On Line." *Chronicle of Higher Education,* July 18, 1997, p. A21.

Paine, N. "The Role of the Community College in the Age of the Internet." *Community College Journal,* 1996, *67* (1), 33–37.

Roueche, J. E., Taber, L. S., and Roueche, S. D. *The Company We Keep: Collaboration in the Community College.* Washington, D.C.: American Association of Community Colleges, 1995.

Senge, P. M. *The Fifth Discipline: The Art and Practice of the Learning Organization.* New York: Currency Doubleday, 1990.

Seymour, D. "The Baldrige Cometh." *Change,* Jan.–Feb. 1994, pp. 16–27.

Shreve, D. L. "Block Grants: The View from the Dome." *Community College Journal,* 1996, *66* (4), 24–26.

Wheatley, M. J. *Leadership and the New Science: Learning About Organization from an Orderly Universe.* San Francisco: Berrett-Koehler, 1992.

Zeiss, T., and Associates. *Developing the World's Best Workforce: An Agenda for America's Community Colleges.* Washington, D.C.: American Association of Community Colleges, 1997.

WILLIAM BERGQUIST *is owner of The Professional School of Psychology, Sacramento, California, and an independent consultant in Gualala, California.*

An annotated bibliography on organizational change is provided. It includes publications on models of change, case studies, and general articles.

Sources and Information on Organizational Change in the Community College

Elizabeth Foote

Change in community college organization is inevitable; as noted earlier in this volume, community colleges are predisposed to transformation. They constantly make and remake themselves in response to social, economic, and governmental transformations. However, change can be controlled and managed, as the following documents illustrate.

The materials reviewed in this article reflect the current ERIC literature on organizational change. These citations offer information on practical models for managing organizational change and case studies of community colleges that have undergone change.

Most ERIC documents (publications with ED numbers) can be viewed on microfiche at approximately nine hundred libraries worldwide. In addition, most may be ordered on microfiche or on paper copy from the ERIC Document Reproduction Service (EDRS) at (800) 443–ERIC. Citations preceded by an asterisk (*) refer to journal articles that are not available from EDRS. Journal articles may be acquired through regular library channels or purchased from one of the following article reproduction services:

Carl Uncover: http://www.carl.org/uncover/, uncover@carl.org, (800)787–7979
UMI: orders@infostore.com, (800) 248–0360
ISI: tga@isinet.com, (800) 523–1850.

General Articles

*Alfred, Richard L., and Carter, Patricia. "Out of the Box: Strategies for Building High-Performing Colleges." *Community College Journal,* 1997, 67 (5), 41–44.

The authors argue that current changes in the educational climate require transformations in community college organization. They discuss operational, linear, and framebreaking approaches to change that are important in making the transformation to high-performing institutions or that manage both incremental and revolutionary change.

Harris, Zelema M. "Institutional Transformation." Paper presented at the 101st Annual Meeting of the North Central Association of Colleges and Universities, Chicago, Mar. 23–26, 1996. 22 pp. (ED 405 042)

Although incivility and conflict have long plagued community colleges and other educational institutions, recent budget declines have made this situation more critical. It is important that the institutions be transformed and that civility, caring, and respect be infused into the organization. Specifically, traditional singular leadership should be replaced by collective leadership, with traditional middle managers being replaced by management teams, and efforts should be made to include the voices of women, minorities, and other traditionally silenced groups in the organizational dialogue. Although deep structural transformation takes time, the following nine nonlinear stages of the transformation process have been identified: (1) understanding the organizational structure, (2) articulating the institution's vision, (3) creating an environment of trust, (4) easing the threat of change, (5) using information to transform institutions, (6) moving away from hierarchical models of management, (7) providing opportunities for faculty and staff development, (8) creating an inclusive environment, and (9) evaluating managers' personal values.

Models

Models can offer guidelines for administrators facing organizational change. The following are a sample of recently devised models.

Frank, Debra, and Rocks, William. "Exploiting Instability: A Model for Managing Organizational Change." In *The Olympics of Leadership: Overcoming Obstacles, Balancing Skills, Taking Risks.* Proceedings of the 5th Annual International Conference of the National Community College Chair Academy, Phoenix, Ariz., Feb. 14–17, 1996. Phoenix: National Community College Chair Academy, 1996. 8 pp. (ED 394 564)

In response to decreased levels of funding and declining enrollments, increased competition, and major technological advances, Allegany Community College, in Maryland, has developed a model for managing organizational change. The model incorporates the following four components for effective transition and change: conceptualization, communication, commitment, and control systems. Conceptualization involves understanding that the different parts of the organization are integrated into a whole and recognizing that change perceived as negative for one area may actually be positive for the college. Cross-college representation on most committees and task forces provides individuals with the opportunity to view change from others' perspectives. The second component, active, two-way communication, is a powerful adjunct to traditional communication and can help make change happen. Effective communication is a prerequisite to changing attitudes and behavior and is vital to fundamental organizational change. The third component, the commitment of all personnel to strategic planning and their input in that process, is an integral part of organizational growth and development. Any hope of commitment to change, however, must begin with frank discussion of possible causes of resistance and change. Finally, management systems and support services that are dedicated to managing change and monitoring progress in the change process must be created. Organizational leaders should be sensitive to managing change and deploying resources and expertise to assist in transitions.

Levin, Bernard H., and others. "Strategic Planning in a Decentralized Environment: The Death of Linearity." Paper presented at the 24th Annual Conference of the Southeastern Association for Community College Research, Asheville, N.C., Aug. 6–9, 1995. 30 pp. (ED 385 308)

Although private industry has been decentralizing for the past decade, community colleges have been slow to follow. For those colleges that have decentralized, traditional structured planning methodologies do not apply. Although a formal model for planning in a decentralized institution would inhibit change and be counterproductive, the following ideas can be taken into consideration: (1) an institution must analyze its own identity and functions, rather than rely too heavily on ideas from the corporate sector, (2) routine processes ought to be reengineered only when appropriate, (3) institutions must buy into the notion of widescale collaboration, (4) evolution is normal and is the outcome of decentralized strategic planning, (5) college members must be willing to yield to broader concerns even as they recognize that institutional interests sometimes conflict with their own, (6) an ongoing planning process is desirable and necessary, (7) there must be a large and widely shared information base, (8) planners should avoid limiting recommendations based on perceptions of the resources likely to become available, and (9) barriers within the existing structure should be razed. Since 1989, Virginia's Blue Ridge Community College has experimented with a decentralized approach, and the first decentralized strategic plan was published in 1991.

Mellow, Gail O. "The Role of the Community College Chair in Organizational Change: Chaos, Leadership and the Challenge of Complexity." Paper presented at the 2nd Annual Mid-Atlantic Community College Chair/Dean Conference, Blue Bell, Pa., Oct. 24–25, 1996. 25 pp. (ED 401 970)

The hierarchical organizational structures that exist at community colleges and other institutions of higher education reflect the Late Industrial Era; as organizations make the transition to the Early Information Era, however, these rigid structures can hinder institutions' efforts to effectively utilize information and respond to changing conditions. What is needed is a system that merges the process of faculty decision making with a bureaucratic system of student registration and admissions. One possible model of this structure is the learning organization, or a structure that allows for learning and change at the organizational level, enables stability in dynamic environments, generates abundant information, and processes information rapidly. In working toward this model, academic chairs must be able to inspire their faculty to change, imagine the whole system, understand the mental models on which processes are built, and encourage dialogue. Another concept useful in considering structural change is coevolution, or the ability of two systems to interact and grow over time. Key to coevolution is communication; academic administrators need to find ways to increase communication to achieve a rich dialogue and encourage systems to mutually evolve.

Parsons, Michael H. "Gifts Differing: Critical Reflection, Technology and the Creation of a Learning Culture." Paper presented at the 10th Annual Conference of the Eastern Regional Competency-Based Education Consortium, Charleston, S.C., Mar. 12–14, 1997. 12 pp. (ED 405 915)

Critical reflection refers to an adaptation of civic literacy theory by educators seeking to promote the development of learning communities, taking an analytical approach to educational institutions. Critical reflection is being combined with the praxis approach, which stresses investigating issues, acting on the basis of findings, subjecting outcomes to personal reflection, and reapplying the cycle, to develop a learning culture in which teachers act as guides and assessors. As compelling as learning culture theory is, however, it will have little effect without a design for systemic change that involves the following five key institutional systems: communications, professional development, mission redefinition, educational delivery, and self-correction. Further, a five-stage model has been developed for involving all constituents in the process of designing a learning culture that includes telling stakeholders of benefits, selling the vision, testing the new vision and mission statements, consulting with stakeholders, and co-creating the new mission with stakeholders. The change process must be able to adapt coherently to unpredictable environmental conditions, cope with complex systems and limited funding, and develop flexible response systems.

Spanbauer, Stanley J. *Reengineering Education with Quality: Using Quality Concepts, Techniques, and Tools to Improve Education.* Indianapolis, Ind.: USA Group National Quality Academy, 1996. 175 pp. (ED 397 915; not available from EDRS: order from USA Group National Quality Academy, N615 Communication Drive, Suite 2A, Appleton, WI 54915–8593, for $21 plus $3.95 shipping and handling.)

Designed to assist educators in formulating Total Quality Improvement (TQI) plans, this book examines the processes of TQI, which allow for the review of college administration, student services, teaching, and institutional culture, and it provides information on its implementation at two-year colleges. Chapter 1 describes background to educational reform in general and provides a rationale for introducing TQI into educational settings. Next, chapter 2 suggests that the key element of TQI in education is a focus on the customer and describes the following key components of TQI: leadership, team problem solving, the collection of meaningful data, the use of scientific methods and tools, and the focus on training for development. Leadership and the use of teams are discussed in chapter 3, and chapter 4 explores the use of TQI to improve teaching. The pivotal role of community service in TQI systems is outlined in chapter 5, and chapter 6 provides an overview of assessment methods under TQI, providing an assessment model containing multiple measures of progress and a feedback methods matrix. In chapter 7, brief profiles are presented of eleven two-year institutions that have successfully implemented TQI. Finally, chapter 8 discusses the maintenance of TQI systems. The book contains twenty-nine endnotes and a subject index.

Watwood, Britt, and others. "Managing Organizational Change." In *Walking the Tightrope: The Balance Between Innovation and Leadership*. Proceedings of the 6th Annual International Conference of the Chair Academy, Reno, Nev., Feb. 12–15, 1997. 8 pp. (ED 407 017)

Based on studies comparing leadership in two rural community colleges undergoing change and examining the management of change at Maryland's Allegany College, this paper presents a conceptual framework and model for managing organizational change. The framework points to two expected outcomes of leadership strategies: institutional innovation and constituent satisfaction. Next, implications of the framework are described, stressing the important roles of both presidents and chairs in dealing with change, the importance of staff development, and the need to balance instructional and administrative duties of chairs. Finally, a model for managing organizational change is provided, including the following four components: conceptualization, or recognizing the different parts of a system as a whole, which may best be accomplished through crosscollege representation on committees; active, two-way communication; commitment by leaders to organizational goals to gain the commitment of stakeholders; and the creation of management systems and support services dedicated to managing change and monitoring progress in the change process.

Case Studies

The following case studies are examples of how community colleges have coped with organizational change.

*Cooper, Joanne, and Kempner, Ken. "Lord of the Flies Community College: A Case Study of Organizational Disintegration." *Review of Higher Education,* 1993, *16* (4), 419–437. (EJ 469 055)

An interpretive case study examines the organizational disintegration of a community college that experienced a sudden loss of leadership, focusing on how its culture both contributed to and prevented organizational chaos. It addresses how leaders can honor the culture and mission of educational organizations and simultaneously work to transform them.

Fonte, Richard. "Roles and Responsibilities—Single College Orientation." Paper presented at the 77th Annual Convention of the American Association of Community Colleges, Anaheim, Calif., Apr. 12–14, 1997. 11 pp. (ED 408 003)

Austin Community College (ACC) is undergoing reorganization in an attempt to create a "single college" organizational structure to replace its current "campus with five competing colleges" model. By doing so, ACC hopes to create an atmosphere in which short- and long-range planning efforts are aimed at the overall good of the organization. The three principles of the reorganization are responding to student, faculty, and administrator concerns, becoming more responsive to the local business community with workforce education, and empowering faculty decision making. ACC has restructured the administration, adding two vice presidents and replacing department chairs with seven deans and ninteen or twenty assistant deans drawn from the full-time faculty. In addition, eighteen instructional task forces will have major academic programming responsibilities and will act as a link between the deans and the faculty. Three provosts will oversee multiple colleges, with one overseeing the three geographically close campuses in the central Austin area, another coordinating the growth of two developing campuses, and a third linking the programs of ACC's extension operation with a comprehensive campus.

Gould, Timothy D. "Development of a Strategy for Transition for State Community College from a State Agency to an Independent College." Ed.D. Practicum, Nova Southeastern University. 146 pp. (ED 409 965)

In preparation for a 1996 restructuring at State Community College, in Illinois, from a state agency to an independent community college, a project was undertaken to develop a strategic plan to guide the transition. Specifically, the project sought to determine the necessary elements of and functions and activities required by the plan, appropriate people to be included on transition teams, necessary changes in college operations, and required inservice training for faculty and staff. First, a review was undertaken of literature related to administrative change and planning and a transition management team was appointed. Once committees were developed on the team, strategic plans developed at other colleges that had made similar transitions were reviewed and a plan was developed and revised. The project found that essential elements of the plan were a revitalized mission statement, a set of planning assumptions, assignment of responsibilities, and procedures for evaluation and assessment. With respect to changes in college operations, it was determined that the new organizational structure would represent a 50 percent reduction in staff and faculty and a reduction in administrative positions. The work contains seventy-four references. Appendixes provide a transition management team agenda sheet, the college's mission and vision statement and organizational structure, transition management team presentation documents, an institutional self-assessment instrument, and issues and strategies identified by the project.

Levin, John S. "Presidential Succession and Organizational Change in the Community College. ASHE Annual Meeting Paper." Paper presented at the 21st Annual Meeting of the Association for the Study of Higher Education, Memphis, Tenn., Oct. 31–Nov. 3, 1996. 36 pp. (ED 402 848)

This qualitative study examined the perceived effects of the president on organizational change at five community colleges in one state, and is part of a multiple case study that is addressing organizational change in community colleges. The methodology for the study was based on the literature of organizational change, which suggests four constructs: change in the organizational paradigm, in which underlying assumptions of participants have changed; change in organizational mission and purpose; change in organizational culture; and change in functional processes such as organizational structures, managerial practices, technology, decision making, and communications. Data collection and analysis involved interviews with presidents, administrators, faculty, and support staff; questionnaires; group meetings; and documents. The study found that community college presidents were seen to "make a difference," with the greatest influence being perceived during periods of leadership succession. Organizational changes attributed to presidents are summarized in two tables: the first covers data obtained during interviews and the second summarizes data obtained from the questionnaires.

Sir Sandford Fleming College Repositioning Strategies Report. Peterborough, Ontario: Sir Sandford Fleming College, 1996. 72 pp. (ED 399 978)

This report describes repositioning strategies undertaken by Sir Sandford Fleming College, in Ontario, to respond to changing student demographics, educational demands, and reduced funding. Following opening remarks by the college president providing an overview of the strategies and the use of all-staff meetings to generate responses from the campus community, repositioning strategies are detailed in the areas of (1) academic redesign, including the suspensions and modifications of programs and new techniques for program delivery, (2) financial strategies to reduce program and nonsalary costs and to increase revenue, (3) space consolidation by vacating off-campus facilities during summers, (4) human resources strategies, including an early retirement plan for staff and hiring freezes, and (5) a new organizational structure designed to make the college learner-centered, flexible, and customer-focused. The report provides an overview of organizational attributes under the new structure; key features of the structure, including six centers of specialization and a learning resource center; and a discussion of benefits to students. Finally, appendixes provide a description of desired organizational attributes and design principles guiding the new structure, organizational charts of the college and divisions, a summary of results from a survey of student satisfaction, and a discussion of the role of leadership and teams in the new centers of specialization.

ELIZABETH FOOTE is the user services coordinator at the ERIC Clearinghouse for Community Colleges.

INDEX

Townsend, B., 56
Transfers, 7–8, 32; and Puente Project, 37, 38
Trombley, W., 19, 22
Twombley, S., 83

UMI article reproduction service, 99
Unions, faculty, 50–51
University of California, 37–38; Office of President, 37
University of Minnesota, exclusion of, from merger, 7
Urban areas: changing demographics of, 67–68; effects of changes in, on community colleges, 71; influence of technology on, 67

Valadez, J. R., 32, 34, 35, 36, 81
Van Maanen, J., 32, 33, 34, 36

Virtual organizations, 91, 95
Visions, shared, 61, 63

Waldrop, M. M., 69
Watwood, Britt, 103
Welfare-to-work policies, 3
Wheatley, M. J., 62, 69, 70, 72, 73, 74, 90, 92
White, K. B., 21
Whitt, E. J., 55, 60
Wildavsky, A., 21
Williams, S. K., 81
Wilson, R., 31
Workfare policies, 3
Writing, in Puente Project, 36–37

Zeiss, T., 81, 90, 91, 94
Zohar, D., 69
Zwerling, S. L., 34, 80

Back Issue/Subscription Order Form

Copy or detach and send to:

Jossey-Bass Inc., Publishers, 350 Sansome Street, San Francisco CA 94104-1342

Call or fax toll free!

Phone 888-378-2537 6AM-5PM PST; Fax 800-605-2665

Back issues: Please send me the following issues at $22 each

(Important: please include series initials and issue number, such as CC90)

1. CC _____

_____

_____

$ _____ Total for single issues

$ _____ Shipping charges (for single issues *only;* subscriptions are exempt from shipping charges): Up to $30, add $5^{50} • $30^{01}–$50, add $6^{50} $50^{01}–$75, add $7^{50} • $75^{01}–$100, add $9 • $100^{01}–$150, add $10 Over $150, call for shipping charge

Subscriptions   Please ❏ start   ❏ renew my subscription to *New Directions for Community Colleges* for the year 19___ at the following rate:

❏ Individual $57   ❏ Institutional $107

NOTE: Subscriptions are quarterly, and are for the calendar year only. Subscriptions begin with the spring issue of the year indicated above. For shipping outside the U.S., please add $25.

$ _____ Total single issues and subscriptions (CA, IN, NJ, NY and DC residents, add sales tax for single issues. NY and DC residents must include shipping charges when calculating sales tax. NY and Canadian residents only, add sales tax for subscriptions)

❏ Payment enclosed (U.S. check or money order only)

❏ VISA, MC, AmEx, Discover Card #_____ Exp. date_____

Signature _____ Day phone _____

❏ Bill me (U.S. institutional orders only. Purchase order required)

Purchase order #_____

Name _____

Address _____

_____

Phone_____ E-mail _____

For more information about Jossey-Bass Publishers, visit our Web site at:

www.josseybass.com   **PRIORITY CODE = ND1**

OTHER TITLES AVAILABLE IN THE
NEW DIRECTIONS FOR COMMUNITY COLLEGES SERIES
Arthur M. Cohen, Editor-in-Chief
Florence B. Brawer, Associate Editor